HAND BLOCK PRINTING
& RESIST DYEING

HAND BLOCK PRINTING & RESIST DYEING

Susan Bosence

DAVID & CHARLES
Newton Abbot   London

(*frontispiece*) One side of author's London
exhibition 1961 (*John Donat*)

*Photographs show the work of the author unless
otherwise attributed
Line drawings by David Hayes*

British Library Cataloguing in Publication Data

Bosence, Susan
  Hand block printing and resist dyeing.
  1. Dyes and dyeing, Domestic   2. Textile
printing
  I. Title
  746.6   TT853

  ISBN 0-7153-8524-0

Second impression 1991

Typeset by Typesetters (Birmingham) Ltd,
Smethwick, West Midlands
and printed in Great Britain
by Butler & Tanner Limited, Frome and London
for David & Charles
Brunel House Newton Abbot Devon

CONTENTS

Plate 1 Interior of Barron and Larcher's house at Painswick, 1963 (*Dietrich Hanff*)

FOREWORD

This book is a rare event because it is written by a distinguished artist craftsman who since the 1950s has been a printer and dyer of cloth. Susan Bosence shares with us the steps in the development of her own work and her view of textile artists of other periods and cultures. The book encourages those who have already embarked on this kind of discovery and will inspire others to start. Let us hope it will increase the appreciation of hand-patterned cloth.

In the first half of the twentieth century in England there were few artist craftsmen printing and dyeing cloth, compared to the number of potters and weavers. Printed cotton had become a cheap commodity in the nineteenth century, as it had been one of the first materials to be affected by mass production in the industrial revolution, with an increasing separation between designer and maker. William Morris had reacted so strongly against this that in the 1880s he went to great lengths to set up a workshop for block printing and dyeing cloth with indigo, madder and weld. His legacy was perhaps too strong. His designs, printed in the authentic colours and methods, continued to be available into the 1920s and 30s but, by then, were quite out of keeping with the design ideas of the period. The Omega Workshop led the new mood of abstraction but showed little understanding of dyes in their fabrics. However the interest in simple bold designs encouraged a climate in which artists could attempt to produce their own fabrics. The painters, Phyllis Barron and Dorothy Larcher, who started printing fabrics in the 1920s, achieved the best balance between contemporary imagery and high standards of methods and material. They rediscovered for themselves the early cloths and dyes that had inspired William Morris, although they had no love for the Morris and Co fabrics.

It was Barron and Larcher who, in the 1950s, encouraged Susan Bosence in her first diffident steps in printing and who passed on to her their knowledge of dyes. They introduced her to Muriel Rose, a person of great discrimination who was vital in the promotion of crafts. Her first patrons were Dorothy and Leonard Elmhirst, the founders of the splendid pioneer community at Dartington in Devon to which Susan and her husband belonged, and which was a wonderfully nourishing environment for many creative artists and teachers. Susan was involved in Robin Tanner's memorable Ministry of Education courses at Dartington to which teachers came from all over England.

The importance of Susan Bosence in the history of twentieth-century craft is due to the quality of her work and her influence as a teacher. Students of all ages came to her workshop at Dartington from 1960 to the early 70s and from the late sixties Susan taught in the Textile Departments of Camberwell College of Art in London and the West Surrey College of Art and Design, Farnham, where she is still a valued part-time teacher. She herself has not sought the limelight. There has been one major exhibition of her work in London in 1961 but since then, except for participation in a few mixed exhibitions, Susan has shown her work in the Westcountry in Bath, Carmarthen, Bristol and Totnes. Readers of this book may like to know that the Trustees of the Crafts Study Centre at the Holburne of Menstrie Museum, Bath, have had the foresight to build a collection of her textiles.

It is vital however to realise that Susan's work is in no way 'museum art'. Her textiles are made for use, for clothes or in the home. Their scale is chiefly domestic and they belong to a world of natural beauty. They associate happily with stone, wood and plants. They look their best in natural light, creating a mood of quiet harmony. The cloths, mostly cotton, some silk, have an apparent simplicity of pattern. Each mark, whether printed, waxed, pasted or stitched, tells of the hand that has made it, so there is a vitality and subtlety at the same time. Designing is for Susan an experience with the cloth so that her initial inspiration becomes manifest in dyes, marks, cloth. She says of herself that she is not a cerebral person but a simple doer 'relating what I see, to what I do and vice versa'. She takes great trouble to find cloths of character as her raw material. It is significant that she likes unbleached calico because it has no 'make-up'. She says 'the final piece of cloth should be a whole piece of cloth – the quality of the cloth, the colour and the pattern of equal standard, lovely to look at, handle and use'.

This book is not a blueprint for the creation of textiles. It cannot be or it would be suffocating. But it is an invitation to share an approach and an aim of creating beauty in textiles that speak in their own terms and are true to their maker. As a teacher Susan Bosence has always encouraged students to explore something outside themselves and then to transmute this into cloth form. It is important to communicate something, not to experiment for experiment's sake. One main message comes through as well; the use of dyeing techniques helps to develop an awareness of the cloth as a whole. Susan Bosence is a superb dyer and printer and we would do well to follow her advice; to see how she organises her workshop and how she has looked and learnt and is still learning. We are lucky that she has been ready in this book to share so much experience with a wide audience.

DERYN O'CONNOR

INTRODUCTION

We came to work at Dartington, Devon, in the late thirties. The Hall, a partly ruined medieval manor house, was bought in the twenties by Leonard and Dorothy Elmhirst, in pursuit of an ideal – to revive the economic, social and cultural life of the countryside which had suffered a serious decline, and to lay the foundations for study and research in education, agriculture and the arts. The manor house and buildings were faithfully restored by master builders, stone dressers and tilers, and enterprises for farming, horticulture, forestry, sawmilling and textiles were set up, followed by a co-educational boarding school and arts centre. All this was flourishing in the years before World War II, though during the War its activities were of course seriously curtailed. In spite of the drastic upheavals of that time, Dartington survived and exists today as a unique centre for the arts, crafts and education; also for various industrial and rural activities, including a glass factory, horticultural training, forestry, cattle breeding, and numerous other enterprises.

The work of the school and the arts department, and the surrounding beautiful countryside and buildings have made a lasting impression on me, and I remain deeply grateful for all the interest and support shown to me by the Elmhirsts and many others on the estate.

One day in the early fifties Dorothy Elmhirst invited me to see some printed cottons and linens which she had chosen for furnishing rooms in the Hall and School at Dartington. There were rich blues, subtle browns and reds, ochres and smokey blacks, in simple patterns on linens, fine cambrics and calicos. They seemed exactly right for the Devonshire stone and timber buildings where they were to be used. They had been hand block printed by Phyllis Barron and Dorothy Larcher, who were practising the craft of block printing to a high standard – a standard comparable to the work of other contemporary British pioneers such as Bernard Leach and Michael Cardew (potters), Gimson and Gardiner (furniture makers), and Ethel Mairet and Elizabeth Peacock (spinners and weavers).

These textiles were a revelation to me after the muddled designs and imitation 'chintzes' of the forties. They possessed an affinity with the house we were to live in, with its barn foundations, whitewashed stone walls and wooden floors. Unfortunately, we couldn't possibly afford them, so I resolved to find out how to make some simple versions myself. This has led to years of studying printed and dyed textiles and the nature of dyestuffs, and to the setting up of my own printing and dyeing workshop. Whereas Barron and Larcher worked exclusively with blocks and dyes, I became distracted and seduced by resist and discharge styles, chiefly with indigo, using both ancient and modern chemical dyes. Barron remonstrated in a letter, 'I can only say that I feel your very slow methods of wax and paste resists, all put on by hand, much more laborious than printing, and must make very high costs.' Of course she was right.

There were many difficulties in the way of setting up a workshop in those years after the war: we lived out in the country far away from reference libraries, there were no relevant evening classes, with nowhere to go for tuition and three very small children at home. However, encouraged by friends, I gradually managed to collect tools, cloth, pots and pans, and began to experiment. The Elmhirsts heard of this and urged me to visit Barron and Larcher – a most daunting prospect which seemed quite out of the question with children at home, no reliable car and all that distance between us. Nevertheless, I went in a hired car, taking some of my efforts with me. They were welcoming; they showed me their wonderful materials, antique blocks and textiles collected from their travels and hunts in secondhand shops and sales. I marvelled at their beautiful furniture, shelves of chosen pots, glass, jugs and delicate sprays of flowers from their garden. The kitchen was inviting – a pretty table laid for a meal, the walls hung with well-made cooking utensils from Madame Cadec's shop in Greek Street. I was taken around the garden to see lovely unusual plants in pale creamy whites and dark purplish blacks. They told me not to use that awful colour, but to concentrate on this one; to try larger blocks; to make some indigo, and, above all, to read Dr Edward Bancroft's *Philosophy of Permanent Colours* (1813), which I still refer back to.

Visits were exchanged and we became friends. Dorothy Larcher suffered a terminal illness and was almost bedridden when I knew her, but she was always very encouraging and full of sound advice and didn't seem concerned that I'd not had the chance of studying painting, as they had done. She told me how she and Barron used to go together on painting holidays to Barron's sister's cottage in Normandy; and how their tutor, Fred Mayer, had found and bought in a local market a collection of old wood blocks, with patterns cut into them. He thought they would make a good wall decoration and took them home. Barron, apparently, was fascinated, and thought at first they might be for printing wallpaper, but later realised that the scale and style of the patterns resembled the small flowery prints of French countrywomen's aprons and dresses. Barron and Larcher used to buy rolls of a special handwoven blue cloth from an Armenian shop in Hampstead to make their painting overalls, and Barron noticed that a friend's smock (she was an

Plate 2 (*opposite*) Corner of Barron and Larcher's house. Blockprinted linen curtains in *Skate* design by Barron. Flower painting by Dorothy Larcher (*Dietrich Hanff*)

Plate 3 Hand-painted storage tins in Barron's kitchen (*Dietrich Hanff*)

etcher) nearly always had white spots and splashes on it. Wondering whether these marks were caused by the nitric acid she used for etching, Barron tried to cover the block with the acid and print with it on the blue cloth. She didn't realise that the acid should have been diluted and made into a paste suitable for printing, and she nearly ruined the block and the cloth. However, they both became more interested in block printing techniques than in painting. They learnt that this blue was real indigo, and that there was a world of fascinating methods and dyes to be understood.

From her study of Bancroft and old nineteenth-century dyeing and printing manuals by Knecht and Fothergill and William Crookes, Barron was able to set up a small workshop, tackle the indigo vat, the iron-mould print and dye processes, and make soft blacks with iron and oak galls. At first Ethel Mairet helped to sell their work, and during the twenties and thirties their flourishing and unique workshop produced some of the loveliest hand block printed linens, cambrics, silks and velvets ever made.

Later on, the war curtailed their supply of good raw materials and dyestuffs. Added to this Dorothy Larcher did not recover from her illness and they had to disband the workshop and pack everything away. Barron felt very lonely and lost but she courageously looked ahead for new interests.

She greatly enjoyed working on the local Council and was a wonderful support and adviser to the Gloucestershire Guild of Craftsmen. She enjoyed coming to my workshop and taught me to make an indigo vat and would have loved to print again had there been an opportunity. We had many outings to exhibitions, craft galleries, gardens, libraries, museums and junk shops. She was always looking for the best and most beautiful things man had made. I learnt most of the good things I know from her and her partnership with Dorothy Larcher, and came to appreciate their mastery and love of their craft. Over the years Barron became one of our closest friends and I am sure I didn't realise fully at the time my good fortune and privilege to have had 'tutorials' with her. I do now, of course, and looking back I can begin to assess the immeasurable inspiration they gave me.

I am indebted to family, friends, my editor, publishers and photographers for their tremendous help, tolerance and patience during the research and compilation of this book. It represents more than thirty years of the great fun and excitement that comes from working and learning with students of all ages; and hours of frustration trying to fathom the mysteries of colour and the art of dyeing. I think back to days at the Dartington Adult Education Centre and College of Art, the Yarner workshop, then Camberwell and Farnham Schools of Art, and my Sigford workshop. I would much rather be working than trying to write a book about it, and without the interest, help and encouragement of all those who shared this with me, I could not possibly have done it.

1 · DYES

Until the middle of the nineteenth century, all our dye colours originated from natural sources: from flowers, trees, insects, shellfish and minerals. They were discovered in many cases by accident; followed by pressing, soaking, pounding, boiling and much trial and error before repeatable formulae could be established. The early dyers slowly accumulated their recipes, often keeping them fiercely secret. They understood the interactions of water, heat, acids, alkalies, air and colouring matters, and so it follows that a basic knowledge of chemistry is necessary to understand what is really taking place when a colour forms in the bucket you are stirring.

Dr Andrew Ure, an eminent nineteenth-century academician and chemist, defined dyeing as:

> an altogether chemical process, requiring for its due explanation and practice an acquaintance with the properties of the elementary bodies, and the laws which regulate their combinations. It is the art of impregnating wool, silk, cotton, etc with colours not removable by washing, or the ordinary usage to which these fibrous bodies are exposed.

A true dye therefore cannot be removed from the material by the same process as was used to put it in, ie, the process cannot be reversed.

Phyllis Barron used real dyes, an interest which arose from her investigations into the use of indigo, and later iron rust, cutch and various other plant dyes for cotton and linen. She learnt and understood the basic chemistry through working with them and cloth whilst studying the old dye manuals. This invaluable approach to dyeing and printing was passed to me and formed the basis of my work and interests. Of the many dyestuffs used before the introduction of anilines there

is room here only to discuss those of personal use and interest. The sources of other 'natural' dyes and colours can be found in the books listed in the Bibliography.

Two of the most important ancient dyestuffs are indigo for blue (derived from plants of the *Indigofera* family), and madder for reds, purples, violets and browns (from *Rubia tinctorum*). These two colours originated from plants growing in hot climates where the sun's heat and rich vegetation contribute to strong, vibrant colours in plants and animal life. We learn that the art of dyeing and cotton printing originated over two thousand years ago in India, where indigo, madder and the cotton plant *Gossypium* are found in abundance, together with other mineral substances essential to the dyeing operations. In the British Isles there is a tradition of wool and flax spinning, dyeing and weaving, but cotton is not a native plant, nor are there suitable indigenous dyestuffs for cotton. In nature, compatible fibres and dyestuffs appear in approximately similar situations, and natural dyestuffs tend to echo the colours of their original environment. The traditional colours of Britain are subdued (though varied) yellows, golds, browns and soft blacks.

This chapter introduces these earlier colours, and in later sections there are references to their adaptation to block printing and resist dyeing.

Indigo

Indigo, the historic blue, long ago known as indicum, was principally extracted from species of *Indigofera*, *Isatis*, *Polygonum* and *Nerium*. These plants flourish in hot, wet climates, eg, Africa, India, the Americas, Egypt and the Far East, where the cotton plant also grows. Over the centuries man has

Indigo plant (*Indigofera tinctoria*)

Cotton plant (*Gossypium hirsutum*)

learnt to extract a blue dye from the indigo plant and spin a thread from the filamentous down of the cotton seed, which together make the traditional blue-and-white combination which has continued to the present day, especially for everyday working clothes.

Nowadays indigo comes to us in the form of grains or powder, but the theory of dyeing differs little from early methods when the whole plant was used, and this is a very good reason for studying its early history which illuminates the tedious processes which later led to the modern synthesis. Detailed accounts can be studied in the old manuals listed in the Bibliography, and the following may give some indication of what was involved.

Plant indigo dyeing

The blue colouring matter found in the genera mentioned above is principally in the juice of the leaves. In its natural state it is a white substance which remains white as long as the leaf remains perfect. As soon as the leaf tissue is damaged this white substance absorbs oxygen from the air and turns blue, but it cannot in this simple state be fixed upon cloth as a dye; it will not dissolve in water. It is difficult to imagine how the necessary process was discovered. Perhaps somehow, where a fire had been made, where there were rotten plants and human urine, that blue liquid, if accidentally splashed on cloth would have proved obstinate to remove. We now know why: the urine helped to further the fermentation of the plants, thereby releasing oxygen, and the indigo in this 'reduced' (deoxygenated) state would have been dissolved by the alkali of the wood ashes. M. Hellot, a French dye chemist of the eighteenth century, wrote:

> There is a cold preparation of an indigo vat with urine, and it is worked cold. For this method you take four pounds of powdered indigo, put into a gallon of vinegar, leaving it to digest over a slow fire for four and twenty hours. At the expiration of this time, if it is not perfectly dissolved, it is again pounded in a mortar with the liquor adding now and then a little urine. You then put into it half a pound of madder, mixing it well by stirring the whole with a stick. When this preparation is finished

you pour it into a cask containing sixty gallons of urine: it is of no consequence whether it be stale or fresh.

There follows a Hot Indigo Vat with Urine with even more incredible quantities of the liquid 'made very HOT but without boiling', and the 'scum which rose on the surface of the urine was brushed off the copper with a besom'.

And then there is a very old Shetland recipe used for fisher folks' jerseys which was guaranteed absolutely fast:

> Preserve a gallon of urine for over a fortnight (male urine is best) preferably in a warm place, stir occasionally, and in this soak 1½oz powdered indigo tied in a muslin cloth. Soak wool in warm urine for ten minutes before putting in the tub – which should be kept warm and stirred occasionally. It takes two weeks to get a really good blue.

Plant indigo dyeing in Nigeria

There is a long tradition of indigo dyeing in this part of Africa, where there is an abundance of wild plants which produce indigo. The leaves of the young *Elu* plant (the indigenous *Lonchocarpus*) are collected and pounded to a blue/black mass, then rolled by hand into balls, and left to ferment and dry in the sun. Later, these are dissolved in liquid lye, made by filtering well water through the ashes of carefully burned wood (some old and some green). This becomes the vatting liquid. When judged ready, the balls are broken and slowly added to the dye pot which is then left to stand for about three days, occasionally being stirred. When the dye has matured and is judged ready, the cloth is immersed, soaked well and then lifted out of the pot. At this stage it is of a greenish-yellow colour which gradually turns to blue in the air as the reduced indigo in the vat takes back from the air the oxygen it needs to form indigo blue on the cloth. This process is more fully explained in *Adire Cloth in Nigeria* (see Bibliography) and we return to it in Chapter 8.

Plate 4 shows an indigo dyer in Zebid, in North Yemen, which has always been a most important indigo dyeing centre, and still had about a hundred and fifty indigo dyeing workshops in production in the early 1950s.

The dye was extracted from the plant *Indigofera tinctoria* which was widely cultivated until the revolution of 1962. Synthetic indigo is now used with traditional local ingredients for the vat. These are the melted down leaves of the *Aloe*, the soda made from the burnt trunks of the salt bush *Sueda monorca*, young dates, gum arabic, and resin from *Acacia ehrebergiana* for starch. This last helps to stiffen the cloth and bind the indigo to it. Cloth is beaten until stiff, to make it windproof, by men working in pairs with heavy wooden mallets. The Yemeni welcome the rub-off and believe it is good for the skin and the hair.

In Europe and the West in the eighteenth century, indigo blue became a fashionable colour, which was used increasingly in textile printing. The following thirteen shades of blue were recorded in common use in the trade, beginning with the lightest: white blue, pearl blue, pale blue, faint blue, delicate blue, sky blue, queen's blue, turkey blue, king's blue, garter blue, persian blue, aldego blue, and infernal blue!

Factory production increased — in 1692 there were only sixty indigo plantations in Jamaica, but by 1787 there were 3,150 in San Domingo alone. The cultivation and processing of indigo blue was an essential part of the continuing successful rise of textile printing and dyeing trades through almost to the end of the nineteenth century, when chemists were accelerating their efforts to understand the problems of iron and steam. In 1856 the first synthetic dye was invented, and in 1897 Dr Alfred Baeyer, a German chemist, found a synthesis for indigo blue in a coal-tar product. This had grave consequences for the indigo traders, causing cultivators and manufacturers in the processing plants to lose fortunes. Hundreds of indigo planters were forced to abandon their crops and, gradually, to introduce sugar plantations as a substitute. The making of indigo on a factory scale spread rapidly in the West, and large chemical firms were established, producing indigo in the form of grains or powder. The method now in general use is that for the hydrosulphite vat, which will be explained in detail in Chapter 8. There are those who feel that the final colour is not the same, but we should remember that when the whole plant was employed certain interesting impurities found their way into the vat — weeds, soil, bugs etc — thereby producing a livelier colour. It is certainly true in ceramics, for example, that the so-called 'impurities' resulting from a wood-fired kiln add great interest and depth, whereas the pure factory-made article can appear uniform and dull.

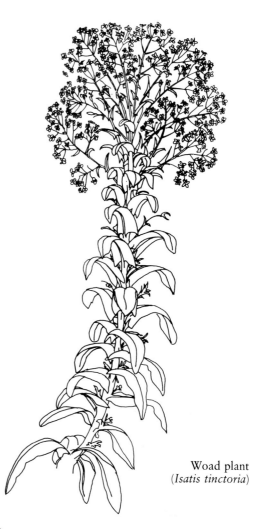

Woad plant
(*Isatis tinctoria*)

Plate 4 Indigo dyeing at Beit Abud, Zebid, in the Red Sea coastal plain (the Tihamah) of North Yemen (*Jenny Balfour-Paul*)

Woad Blue

The indigo colouring matter is also found in the woad plant (*Isatis tinctoria*) which grows wild in Europe, the Americas and Britain. In 1823 an American chemist, William Partridge, wrote:

> To colour a permanent blue is the most difficult process in dying. All other colours may be done by a receipt, and when once well performed may be repeated with the utmost certainty, provided the water and dying wares are the same; but it is not so with woad dying, in this a constant judgment is required. It depends altogether on a given stage of fermentation being equally and constantly preserved, and as this is ever liable to vary from a variety of causes, the operation is thereby rendered very difficult.

The blue dye from the Isatis plant is the *glastum* of the ancients, and this blue has been used on skin and clothes ever since. Pliny recorded how the women of Brittany rubbed woad on their bodies on festival days and walked quite naked, and Caesar wrote of the ancient Britons using it on their faces to appear more terrible in battle.

In Elizabethan times the woad plant was cut, washed and partly dried, taken to a mill and ground to a paste, then left in a heap for a fortnight to ferment. The resulting stench was such that Queen Elizabeth prohibited its manufacture. However, owing to its value as a dye (it gave a stronger and more permanent blue than indigo) its continued (no doubt modified) use lasted well into the twentieth century, when blue 'serge' cloths were made for official uniforms for the post and police etc.

The most important book on Woad is by J. B. Hurry, *The Woad Plant and its Dye* (see Bibliography).

Madder Red

Madder is the wonderful rich and varied red of old Indian painted chintzes. It is obtained from the dried and pounded roots of *Rubia tinctorum*, native to India, the East and parts

Plate 5 The author, indigo dyeing in her Sigford workshop, Devon, 1983 (*Richard Davies/Crafts Council*)

Madder plant (*Rubia tinctorum*)

of Europe. The best European madder is obtained from *R.palus* (from 'aplustre', marshy ground) grown in old Languedoc and especially in the Camargue in France. This variety was apparently established from plants brought by an Armenian traveller in 1762. In the nineteenth century there were fifty water-powered mills in the Avignon area, supplying the lime water necessary for good colour extraction, and £80 million worth of the plant were ground per annum to produce this beautiful and exceedingly fast colour.

The red colouring matter in the plant's roots is released on heating (think of the red juice from cooking beetroot) though this will not of itself give a permanent colour. The early Indians discovered that alum salts with the madder root extract gave a beautiful fast red; iron salts enabled them to make purples and violets, and a mixture of iron and alum gave browns and black, according to the proportion of the salts to the extract. These mineral salts, later known as 'mordants' (Fr *mordre* to bite) unite chemically with the madder extract and form a permanent bond between it and the cloth fibres.

Later, the early Indians extended their trials to make a paste of suitable thickening material to mix with the mordants. By applying this to pre-determined areas, they achieved 'localised dyeing'. Indeed, with this method many colours could be made from immersion in a single dye-bath, and this is the magic which Pliny the Elder saw and recorded on his travels in the East.

This is a brief outline of the madder process used for the early painted calicos and similar styles right through to the middle of the nineteenth century. In India the processes involved took months to complete.

Turkey Red

This madder root process came to Europe from the East and produces what is perhaps the most permanent dyestuff known. The recipe is an adaptation of the Indian one and includes alternate oilings and saltings of the cloth over a period of at least four weeks prior to dyeing – seventeen processes in all. It was one of the great dyeing techniques of history and was used mainly for dyeing plain red cottons and linens, not for printing. Later, a discharging formula was invented which enabled white patterns to be made on a dyed ground. This was eagerly sought after by Europeans but it was not until 1747 that it reached Rouen, from where, in 1785, Pierre Papillon took it to Glasgow. There, a turkey-red dyeing industry, including an immense export trade, flourished for over a hundred years. The Royal Scottish Museum in Edinburgh possesses pattern books from the United Turkey Red Company dating from 1837 to the 1930s.

The ingenious method of bleaching out certain red areas to white was invented there to reproduce the red and white spotted handkerchief styles, the 'bandhanas' of India. The process used two identical perforated lead plates between which the red cloth was firmly engaged and clamped. Then a discharging liquor was passed through the holes in order to bleach out the red dye, giving a pattern of white spots on a red ground. The original Indian bandhanas were produced by tying exceedingly small areas of white cloth prior to the madder dye bath.

The Scottish industry was forced to end when in 1868 a synthesis for madder red (Alizarine) was invented. This, unfortu-

nately, is much too lengthy and complicated a recipe for me to attempt, though Barron and Larcher tackled it at one time.

Yellow

A yellow dye was, and still can be, obtained from many plants and trees and does not need the difficult processes necessary for indigo and madder dyeing. In the hotter climates a large selection of strong yellows are obtainable by simply boiling up tree barks and leaves; eg, peach leaves in Greece and the Eastern Mediterranean countries,

Weld plant
(*Reseda luteola*)

selected trees of Indonesia, and the stigma of saffron crocus of Austria, Spain and southern France (100,000 stigma were necessary to produce a pound of saffron, hence its exclusivity).

The most important yellow in Europe and Britain was made from weld (*Reseda luteola*), a variety of mignonette, which grew profusely. It was considered superior to all other natural yellow colouring matters for fastness to light and to washing, as was reported by Knecht and Lowenthal in 1893. Like madder, it gave different colours according to the mordant used, eg, with chrome it gave an olive-yellow; with alum, a greenish yellow; with tin, a bright yellow; with iron, an olive; and with copper, a yellow-olive. The mature plant is harvested into bundles, then finely chopped, placed in a muslin bag and boiled for about half an hour. The bag of weld is then removed, and the mordanted cloth is simmered in the resulting liquid for about another half an hour.

Both weld and woad grew in England, the latter particularly well in East Anglia, where it was used with the weld yellow to obtain 'Lincoln Green'.

Weld was not surpassed until 1775, when Dr Bancroft returned from North America with specimens of the *Quercitron* yellow made from the bark of *Quercus nigra*, an American oak, which gave a splendidly rich and lasting colour. Moreover, this bark extract afforded eight to ten times the amount of colouring matter obtained from the weld plant which was rapidly superseded, even though some dyers still preferred the weld colour.

Mineral Yellow

Yellow and gold colours were also possible from iron salts. The affinity between cotton and the oxides of iron is such that, by simply immersing cotton fabric in water saturated with iron salts, and leaving it exposed to the air, a yellow-gold colour slowly develops. Perhaps this was first noticed by women who washed their linen in streams which flowed through iron stone deposits, and then left a pile of linen for some time on the banks before rinsing out. The gold colour (which is

iron mould) can also be formed when iron rust is in contact with an alkali. This used to happen accidentally in the days of galvanised iron wash tubs, when the action of alkaline soap on the slightly rusty iron would cause indelible gold marks. This chemical action has been adapted to make a printing paste and a dye bath. Its use and recipes will be found in Chapter 7.

Mineral Browns and Blacks

There are two mineral-salt colours which I have enjoyed using for both printing and dyeing: they are manganous chloride and permanganate of potash.

Manganous chloride is an old mineral salt recipe for dark, rich browns, very fast to light and washing, which can be dyed along with iron rust and for overprinting on indigo. In the old dyebooks it is sometimes referred to as 'manganese bronze' or 'bistre'. Nowadays it is supplied in the form of pink crystals but it is very hygroscopic, ie, when exposed to the air it very soon liquefies and later solidifies. It can be made into a print paste, a dye bath, or can be discharged with an acid (see Chapter 7).

Permanganate of potash gives a softer, greyer brown, and is supplied in purple crystals. It is a powerful oxidizing agent and was used (perhaps still is) in commerce as a bleaching agent. It proves an excellent stain for wood and has antiseptic qualities. Grandmother used it as a disinfectant for sinks, drains and to ward off bugs and aphids in her garden. We were told to gargle with it to keep away throat infections! However, it can nowadays be employed in ways which give good practice in the art of dyeing (see Chapter 6).

Tree Browns and Blacks

Tree barks were extensively used in the East (in particular for the rich tans and browns of Javanese batik cloths), Europe and the Americas for all shades of browns. Bark extracts for dyeing browns and blacks were imported well into the twentieth century. However, since I have never found the time to explore their use, recipes will have to be taken from dye manuals mentioned in the Bibliography.

Primitive people made use of what was available for decoration and their blacks were concocted from soot, smoke and dark muds, with no doubt other ingredients. In parts of the world where suitable trees grow, a kind of cloth known as *tapa, masi*, or bark cloth is made for simple garments, mats and decorative uses. In the Pacific islands, Polynesia and other areas of the southern hemisphere, the cloth is made from the inner bark of *Broussonettia papyrifera* (the paper mulberry tree) which in some places is cultivated expressly for cloth making. The trees are cut young and, while still soft, the bark is stripped and soaked, laid on a convex table or block and beaten until it is as thin as required – sometimes reaching five times its original width. Plate 6 shows two tapa cloths with typical black/brown patterns. The black would have been made from soot and oil (the Kauri gum tree gives a good deep colour), the brown from tree extracts. As can be seen in the lighter example, some patterns are stencilled, some blocked. The design on the background cloth could have been made by rubbing it over a raised (relief) pattern made by sewing ribs of leaves or stalks onto a flat base. I have seen some complicated patterns made from dried banana-leaf veins stitched together.

In *Dyes and Dyeing*, Charles Pellow (Professor of Chemistry at Columbia University) surmised that black marks may have been noticed if leaves happened to fall on the golden iron-dyed parts of linen. That may well have been, as many trees and shrubs contain tannic acid. We know now that the chemical action of iron upon tannic acid, and vice versa, produces soft greys, and smokey or deep blacks, according to the strengths of the ingredients. Recipes for both dyeing and printing have been developed (see Chapter 7).

A very good source of tannin comes from the gall nuts growing on oak trees, those on the Alleppo and Turkey oaks being the best. The galls are formed by the female gall wasp who lays an egg in the rind of the young oak

tree. The egg develops in the resulting swelling in the tree, the young insect eats the contents containing the tannin, and then pierces a hole through the shell to escape. The best galls are therefore those which do not have a hole in the side, known commercially as green or blue galls. Those from which the waspling has departed are yellow, lighter, of inferior quality and known as white galls. There are also other less important ones. Human nature being what it is, some traders used to mask the holes with wax.

Cotton and linen have a remarkable affinity for tannin and consequently the acid has been used in many recipes for cotton dyeing.

Dr Ure tells us that, 'Nut-galls, sulphate of iron and gum, are the only substances truly useful in the preparation of ordinary ink.' Here is his recipe:

12 pounds of nutgalls
5 pounds of green sulphate of iron
5 pounds of gum senegal
12 gallons of water

The bruised nutgalls are to be put into a cylindrical copper, of a depth equal to its diameter, and boiled, during three hours, with three fourths of the above quantity of water, taking care to add fresh water to replace what is lost by evaporation. The decoction is to be emptied into a tub, allowed to settle, and the clear liquor being drawn off, the lees are to be drained.

Soledon and Caledon Dyestuffs

The browns and blacks I use for printing have been made from Soledon dyes, and those for dyeing are from Caledons. These two are not ancient dyestuffs – they were introduced in the early twentieth century – but the dyeing procedures can be likened to those of indigo. By 'vatting' and the reduction and dissolution of the dye in an alkali, a chemical union is formed between cloth and dye. The Soledons are a form of vat dyestuff prepared for printing. This seems an appropriate place to give a little of their history.

After the discovery of aniline dyestuffs in the mid-nineteenth century and the first years of the twentieth, chemists were con-

Plate 6 Two tapa (bark cloths) from Polynesia (*Jonathon Bosley*)

23

cerned with finding acceptable dyestuffs for the growing textile markets. As late as 1900 there were no absolute standards of fastness, and because many of the newly introduced dyes were not very strong to light and washing, people had to take for granted that fabrics would fade. This was not good enough for James Morton, who directed an important Scottish textile company producing high-quality cotton, linen and woollen goods. Having seen some of his firm's tapestries very badly faded after only a week in a shop window, he was so astounded that he began experiments with some of the newly imported vat dyes appearing on the market. He selected those with the highest fastness qualities and used them to dye textiles from his own firm. He sent samples of these to a friend of his living in India asking him to expose them in the blazing sun on the roof of his house there. He was thrilled with the result as the colours had not faded: so the manufacture of Sundour fabrics began (the trade name is from 'sun' and 'dour', an old Gaelic word meaning water). They were at once a great success and were ordered by firms all over the world.

Because of the rising cost of importing the necessary dyes from Europe, Mortons decided to manufacture their own dyes, including some of the chemical ingredients. The intrepid James Morton forged ahead, and the Solway Dye Company was formed, later to become Scottish Dyes Ltd. The final stage in their successful story was the discovery of a suitable process for rendering the Vat series soluble in water, and thus in 1925 Soledon dyestuffs were originated.

Those interested in the chemistry of dyestuffs would enjoy reading *Fast Dyeing and Dyes*, a reprint of a lecture given by James Morton to the Royal Society of Arts in February 1929. Later, Soledon dyes were manufactured by ICI, and procedures for their application are printed in the ICI publication *An Introduction to Textile Printing*.

To date, Soledon dyes are becoming increasingly difficult to obtain, and I am very concerned about the future supply. There is a range of colours from blues, browns, yellows through to greens and reds. As they are very expensive I could afford only two to begin with, and these were Soledon Blue 2 RCS and Brown 3 RS. I used these two colours, and innumerable colour mixes of them, for over two years, enjoying the interest of blue, blue-grey, blue-brown, blue-black and through the browns to soft beige and cinnamon. I approached the choice of a third colour with much thought and finally chose yellow, which enables me to make golds and greens. The Soledon reds presented difficulties, because I had no steamer and because of their tendency to 'bleed'. This can be partly prevented by heating the sulphuric acid bath, but the problems of this outweighed the desire to use the colour. Latterly, I have used Procions to make a red which blends well with the Soledon colours, but as yet I have little experience of the intimate character of many dyes in the Procion range and so do not feel sufficiently well qualified to include them here. Recipes for Soledon and Caledon dyestuffs are in Chapters 7 and 8.

On the subject of colour, I have been strongly influenced by those colours occurring naturally around me in this isolated part of the country, so I feel diffident about using strong, vibrant colour schemes (though I am sometimes very tempted). In southern Europe it would be possible, compelling even to use them, and I do feel this when I am there. Similarly with designs: a visit to London by train or car amid the crowds, buildings, traffic lights, flashing signs, pavements and all that goes with metropolitan life, would surely change one's style. But I have lived in Devon long enough to feel that mine will not change.

2 · LANDMARKS IN BLOCK PRINTING

The dates and origins of block printing are uncertain. There are early examples from the ancient world of simple stamps to press colouring matter or indented pattern onto cloth, clay or plaster. There are records from medieval times of block printing in the Rhineland monasteries, where blackish surface pigments and simple cut blocks were used to decorate roughly woven garments and hangings. In the fourteenth-century book *Libro dell'arte o trattato della pittura* there is a recipe by the Italian Master Dyer Cennino Cennini for dyeing designs on cloth, for embroideries, canopies and banners. In chapter 173 he describes the way to dye (print?) cloth with the help of a wooden pattern (block?). The recipe is for a positive print, using a black obtained by the burning of linseed. The pattern (block) was blackened in the smoke produced by this burning linseed and used to print cloth, which had been damped. Unbleached linen shirts were mostly produced in this way; in Russia they were called 'dymka' from dym, smoke.

It is not the purpose of this book to give a history of block printing, but rather to point to interesting landmarks in its development in the West. In England, renowned for its 'English Chintz', block printing is not an indigenous craft (eg, weaving or pottery), but an imported one with a long and stormy history.

English Calico Printing Industry

This industry grew up following the sea voyages of the sixteenth century when traders brought back shiploads of treasures from the East, including richly patterned textiles. In 1487 Portuguese travellers reached Calicut, in India, and returned with ideas for future trading. Then in 1498 when Vasco da Gama found his new route to the Cape, ships sailed from Europe to trade in spices, precious metals, patterned textiles and loom-state cloth. A trade route to and from the East would include buying cotton goods from India to barter in the Malayan archipelago for spices to take back to Europe.

In 1600, this trading culminated in the foundation of the East India Company, which, thirty years later, was allowed by Royal Proclamation to import Indian textiles. They were known as indiennes, perses, calicuts, pintadoes and chintz – from the Indian word 'chitta' meaning spotted cloth. Pintado is similarly linked with the Portuguese word *pinta* meaning spotted; *pintado*, a spotted hen; and *la pintade*, the guinea fowl of France. These were printed, painted and decorated in elaborate styles employing printing and resist dyeing, as we shall see later.

Until this time in England clothing was rather dull and heavy, made of linen, hemp and wool, and patterned (if at all) with sombre colours. Tapestries and woven silks were of course richer, but there were no handsome lightweight materials for the ladies. The imported textiles from India and the East, beautifully fine muslins and cottons, were an immediate sensation. They were colourful and pretty, with delicate patterns of exotic flowers and birds; and the dyes were fast. In fact, they were quite new and immediately desirable. The demand grew to such proportions that the weavers were seriously losing trade, so in 1700 Parliament was forced to prohibit the imported textiles.

However, in the years leading up to this, William Sherwin, of London, was busy setting up a print and dye works beside the river Lea at West Ham, with the intention of manufacturing adaptations of these Indian goods. He was the first English dyer to master their printing and dyeing techniques, for which he needed to import plain cottons and muslins. He was granted a patent for this purpose for a period of fourteen years. This upset the silk and woollen merchants once more and they induced Parliament to modify the existing Bill prohibiting cotton printing in England on imported cloth. But the demand for Sherwin's goods continued to increase, with consequent welcome employment and profit, so the Bill never became law. Instead, excise duties were imposed, and by 1720 the opposition successfully brought about a new law prohibiting the printing of all-cotton cloth. The battle continued: the printers retaliated by using a mixed cloth of linen warp and cotton weft, and managed to carry on.

Many factories were built near London, and later a very great expansion took place around the northern ports of Lancashire, where small textile trades were already well established (eg the processing of wool and linen imported from Ireland). These Lancashire factories were made possible by the plentiful supply of soft water from springs, streams and rivers flowing from the Pennines. Later, these same waters were to feed the bleaching, fulling and dyeing factories, and provide power for new machinery and steam boilers. The cotton industry gained enormous strength and importance, the weavers gave up struggling and the printing firms resumed the importation of cottons and muslins from the East. The Manchester cotton trade, which led to momentous technical achievements and made many fortunes, was established. Vast mills were built, housing developments planned, and inventions followed for machine spinning, fulling, bleaching and the manufacture of aniline dyestuffs.

We must not forget that the Indian cloths were the initial inspiration and impetus behind these enterprises; that their colours, dye-making and designs were copied; and that, to understand what is referred to as English Chintz, we should return to the original sources and see for ourselves. However good printed reproductions may be, they cannot compare with seeing, and if possible handling, the real thing. There are valuable collections open to the public, worldwide. Go and use them. Make time, wherever you are, to look in museums and costume collections.

In the Indian Section of the Victoria and Albert Museum, London, there is a textile study room and it is possible to make an appointment to visit it and to examine and feel the lovely cloths. Before you go, visit room 41 on the ground floor, and look at the Indian paintings. Notice the charm and exquisite beauty of the people; the delicate treatment of birds, flowers and trees; the minute details of costume, hair arrangements, turbans and jewellery – all in subtle harmony with their surroundings. Still in this gallery, in others nearby and in the textile study room you will find sumptuous silk and wool carpets, printed and appliqué bed covers, hangings, embroidered jackets, jewellery and other adornments. You can feel the sun and splendour. An article from an All India Handicrafts Board pamphlet relates:

The great colour belt in India which is identical with the great printing belt extends from the interior of Sindh through the deserts of Cutch, Kathiawar and Rajputana to the borders of Gujerat. It is as if the fierce sun and bleak stretches of sand have demanded compensation in the deep brilliant colours of clothing. Colours seem to be roasted and matured by the sun. They form a vital part of the background dictated by urges inherent in the environment and the character of the people. As we go further south colours lose their brilliance: they become darker and more subdued till at last they seem to quench themselves in the lush vegetation of the backwaters of Malabar. Practically the whole of this vast colour belt is studded with printing centres and a tradition of resist-dyeing that stretches back a thousand years. In some areas practically every village has its own variation of design, colour and technique. The richest expression in printing was found in the southern areas, taking for inspiration the mural painting in temples.

The wealth of textile arts in the Indian Section and textile study room includes examples of tied, stitched and dyed turban cloths, bedcovers, festival hangings, dresses and embroideries; block-printed scarves and saris; and some of the early hand-painted and resist-dyed calicoes. Notice the beautiful muslins from Dacca known as *Evening Dew* and *Woven Air* – so diaphanous that if laid on the grass they were invisible. The dyers, painters and designers worked from nature, creating fresh and flowing designs. The blockmakers and printers in their turn acquired an equally high standard of craftsmanship. When studying the early cottons, before the patterns were block printed, remember that the delicate leaf stalks, minute details of veining, opening buds and tendrils were all *drawn* by a practised hand. The dyes from plants and minerals produced a harmonious range of rich reds, browns, purples, soft pinks and blues – all enhanced by the creamy background colour. It may be true to say there have never been more delicately beautiful cloths. No wonder they were eagerly sought after by the West and made into the graceful becoming dresses of the eighteenth century. These can be seen in costume collections and perhaps in your local museum there may be treasures brought back from the Raj.

The Origins of Chintz

In the early twentieth century G. P. Baker, an explorer and collector of textiles, travelled extensively among the Indian printers and dyers, collecting accurate information. On his return he published *Calico Painting and Printing in the East Indies* and set up his own now famous firm of G. P. Baker. During the war he stored some precious materials in a trunk in the inspection pit of his garage, but sadly these were damaged by damp and rust. However, they were given to the Victoria and Albert Museum, diligently restored by them, then later shown in an extensive exhibition of Indian chintz at the museum, and also in New York and the Royal Ontario Museum, Toronto, which has a large permanent collection. By appointment you can look at Baker's madder-dyed clothbound portfolio in the Indian Section of the Victoria and Albert Museum. The research for the exhibition was undertaken by John Irwin of the museum, and Katharine Brett of the Royal Ontario Museum, Toronto. Their book, *The Origins of Chintz* (1970), gives detailed accounts of the processes, with over

two hundred photographs of textiles.

There is no room here to explain the entire process. It includes, briefly, successive oilings and beatings of the cloth, then washings and exposure to the sun, prior to the painting in of the design. This is done with a specially made iron 'pen'. The colour is a soft black and is made with an iron solution painted or printed on cloth previously steeped in the juice of myrobalan fruit, which contains an astringent acid. The acid unites with the iron to form the soft black outline. Outlines for areas to be dyed red would be painted or pencilled in with an alum solution which in the dye bath combines with the madder to make red. An iron mordant would be used, and sometimes mixtures of alum and iron, for purples and browns. The yellow would have been developed from tree barks or flowers, and the blue from indigo.

Indigo presented a problem since the colour develops only properly in a dye bath. Consequently it became necessary to wax out all those parts of the cloth which were not intended to be blue. Since only small flowers and leaves were to receive the colour, whole areas had to be resisted out with wax. This was a tremendously lengthy task and it was very difficult to control large pieces of waxed cloth through the dye without causing the wax to crack. There followed the de-waxing and finishing off processes (see Colour Plate 1).

All this is a very long way from ordering by post pots of dye colour, a kitted version of the necessary tools and a book on 'How to Do It'. Armed with these, it is all too easy to have a go, make some hesitant misunderstood efforts and put it all away in a cupboard. It is far better to understand first the origins of the process, and then make a more serious attempt to produce something original, of yourself, with colours you understand.

When you have studied and handled some of the very special Indian chintz and then seen modern versions in shop windows, you may well wonder what has happened. Progress, in the form of increased production, and lack of attention to detail, colour, texture and finish, has inevitably lowered standards. There is an additional factor:

soon after the 'indiennes' appeared on the western market, not all of them suited the English taste for design at the time. Accordingly, 'English' patterns were sent out to India to be adapted for the western trade. The Indian designer in turn, not having his plants and flowers to work from, added his imaginative touches to what became westernised 'exotic chintz'. This became accepted and a thriving cross-breeding continued, resulting in quite unrecognisable hybrid flower forms, infilled with dots, stripes and fancy twirls – a very long way from the empirical painting and drawing of early times. Chintz had become a commercial product, a sad adulteration of the original. Joyce Storey in her *History of Printed Textiles* says:

> The sad thing is that when in the 1920s G. P. Baker did his research for his still unsurpassed survey of Indian chintz he tried to find evidence of the industry lingering on, and by showing the illustrations of old fabrics, sought to recall memories of similar work and methods in the minds of the older people, but failed to do so. In the end all we have managed to do is to kill most of the native skill and to pass on the factory system.

There were, however, some resulting benefits. The complicated interchange of art styles and influences in Europe and America produced some noteworthy individual and sensitive adaptations of Eastern methods. One is reminded of the Dutch interiors displayed in the East India Pepper House Museum at Enkhuisen, Holland. We see a family group, the ladies in overdresses of 'indiennes', the child in simple traditional Dutch handspun and handwoven checks, with stripes of indigo and madder. There are simply patterned tiles on walls and floor, and other Eastern influences, but it all makes an homogeneous group. The colours and textures of these traditional costumes were not conflicting.

Development of the Industry

In Europe we settled down, after the first excitement and flush of Indian imports, to a period of experiment and improvement in home talents. Flower painters and artists were employed to design beautifully drawn sprigs and sprays of flowers, garlands of garden plants and the rose in all her glory. Small block printing firms carried out these designs to an equally high standard. The printers took seven years to master their craft, and the blockmakers achieved remarkable accuracy and skill in cutting these sprigs and details of petals into wood blocks, sometimes adding copper strips for fine lines and metal pins for spots. The blocks were made by specialist craftsmen of several layers of hard wood and measured up to 12in (30cm) square. They were heavy and irksome to use, though the printers achieved a wonderful rhythm of printing and became accustomed to their hard work.

Separate blocks were made, and printed, for each colour. To ensure accurate printing, registration pins were specially placed on or near the corners by the blockmaker, this being one of the most experienced jobs in that workshop.

The tables were up to 24yd (22m) in length, supported on bricks. The tops were covered with a solid mass of concrete, then blankets and a waterproof surface. A backing sheet would be gummed down on top of this and, finally, the material to be printed would be neatly ironed or pinned parallel to the table edge.

One of the problems inherent in block printing is to find a way of covering the surface of the block with dyestuff. From early times, a pad of soft blanket or felt was used to transfer dye to the block. The dye, in paste form, would be brushed evenly on this soft surface, giving a good spread of dye colour. Then the printer could pick up the right amount of dye to make a good impression on the cloth. One cannot obviously print with a liquid dye – it has to be mixed with a thickener to just the right consistency for the design in question, a point which had to be discussed with dye-mixer and printer before the job commenced, eg, some finely cut designs require a thinner or thicker mixture depending on the texture of the cloth to be printed. This is another very vital operation to which attention must be paid.

At some stage, no doubt, a printer felt he could be helped by having someone to replenish the pick-up pad with dye. This avoided putting the block down each time, to take up the brush and spread the dye himself. So, a boy or girl would learn this job. After that, when long lengths of material were to be printed, an assistant with trolley and dye worked alongside the printer. Instead of a blanket pad, a more efficient contraption called a 'tiering tray' was invented, consisting of a square or rectangular bath, a good deal larger than the size of the block, and half-filled with thick gum. On this floated a frame with a suitable material stretched on it to make an even but slightly resilient surface on which the assistant brushed the dye paste.

One slight disadvantage of this tray is that the cloth may sag a little in the middle, causing the block to pick up more dye on the corners than the middle, and resulting in dye catching on the sides of the block. To avoid this, the Crayford Print Works developed a cushioned pad which had a very slightly curved surface for an even spread of dye.

From the 1780s important advances were made in dye technology and printing methods. Whilst wood blocks continued to be used and improved upon, copper-plate methods (begun in 1761) were increasingly employed. Later on, towards the end of the eighteenth century, these in turn were overtaken by the roller printing machines.

Dyers were feverishly experimenting with chemical 'raised' colours – 'whereby an insoluble metallic salt or oxide or an insoluble colour lake is produced and fixed on the fibre at one and the same time by a process of precipitation' (Knecht and Fothergill). Chrome yellow, iron buff, manganese bronze and prussian blue are examples of this method. These colours, some of them pleasant enough singly, were extremely garish in combination. The late Peter Floud of the Victoria and Albert Museum, has said that he thought these colours did more damage to colour development than the aniline dyestuffs discovered by Perkin in 1856.

Perkin was a chemist working with by-products of iron and steam who chanced on an entirely new substance by the action of 'nitrosodimethylaniline and diethylmeta-phenylenediamine'. 'My experiments', he said, 'instead of yielding the colourless quinine (which he was seeking) gave a reddish powder.' To understand this he tried another method, with aniline, and in this case obtained a perfectly black product, which he purified and digested with spirits of wine. Thus, by pure chance, he made the first aniline dye, Mauveine.

Perkin was knighted, enormous chemical colour industries grew up, old dyeing methods were overtaken, manufacture moved to industrial towns, and we were deluged with a bewildering variety of colours from which we have not recovered. In that fervour and excitement some old 'natural' dyestuffs were abandoned, though they could still be retrieved by studying the recipes in old dye manuals (some of which were used by William Morris and Barron and Larcher). There followed a marked deterioration in industrial manufactures. Cheap materials were hurriedly made for quick financial returns in an attempt to rescue trade, but with little success.

In the midst of this, a few block printing firms remained solvent, though their designs and colours lacked the freshness of earlier productions – possibly because the elaboration of techniques and the separation of design work from the actual printers ended in confused interpretations of the artist's original intent. The factory system cannot work in the same way as one man in his family workshop in India, where he had everything under his eye. In a factory there are the designers, whose work is sent to the blockmaking department, whose work is sent on again to the print department, to print with colours that the dye department has mixed. Hence the difficulties facing a firm trying to organise harmonious designs from several workshops. If an artist craftsperson wishes to design and to see the work right through then there is nothing for it but to do everything oneself. This was one of William Morris's ambitions. He had a passionate desire to revive block printing, to give new birth to designs, to draw fresh flowers, trees and birds from his own garden, to make his own cloth and dyes, to turn everything upside down and begin again.

Plate 7 *Evenlode* chintz designed by William Morris, 1883. Indigo-dyed cloth, resist block-printed by Morris and Co at Merton Abbey (*William Morris Gallery, Walthamstow, London*)

Plate 8 *Eyebright* chintz, discharge block-printed in two strengths on indigo-dyed ground. Designed in 1883 by William Morris (*William Morris Gallery, Walthamstow, London*)

Plate 9 *Jasmine* wallpaper, one of William Morris's most original designs, 1872
(*City of Birmingham Museum and Art Gallery*)

William Morris

Unfortunately there is room here only for a look at his work in textiles. In the Bibliography there are books giving accounts of his life and times, of his involvement in the turbulent changes of nineteenth-century society. He was born in March 1834 into a wealthy business family, educated at Marlborough and Oxford where he became implicated in complex religious, political and aesthetic reforms. His close associates were Burne-Jones, Rossetti, Cormell Price and William Faulkner, who shared his love of Ruskin and the pre-Raphaelites. He studied stained glass and wood carving, became an architect, and later founded his own firm of Morris, Marshall, Faulkner and Company. He believed that good decoration, involving the 'luxury of taste rather than that of costliness would be found to be much less expensive than is generally supposed'. He was a contradictory man – he looked backward to the gothic, to medieval art, yet forward to progressive movements. This is shown in his printed textile designs which have their base in stylistic medieval forms with which he skilfully combined his own observational drawings from his garden.

Morris was thirty-nine in 1873 when he began to work seriously on printed textiles. Outside of his group of artists and reformers who wore, of course, 'Reform' dress, what did he see? Fashionable ladies chose patterned muslin, or silk taffeta dresses, flounced, frilled and fringed over crinolines. They had side-laced boots, dainty parasols, and, when they were not transported in carriages, their voluminous skirts swept in the dirt and filth of streets without drains. The ladies in Morris's circle wore, and often made for themselves, simple clothes of flowing lines, reminiscent of the romantic pre-Raphaelites, and Morris himself was faithful to his indigo-dyed shirt and suit.

In industry, roller printing had overtaken copper-plate processes, with worsening results. The Great Exhibition, which Morris thought 'wonderfully ugly', had taken place. Synthetic dyes were being manufactured on a factory scale, but Morris was determined to use the real old colours – indigo blue, madder red, walnut brown and plant yellows. He worked alongside Arthur Wardle, a notable dye chemist, and persevered with the lengthy dyeing procedures. The results can be seen in Kelmscott Manor, where Morris lived at one time, in the Victoria and Albert Museum and at The Water House, Walthamstow. There is a very important collection (the Sanford and Berger) at Stanford University, California, including Morris's dye book from the Merton Abbey printworks. Some private houses have curtains and furnishings from his firm which are still in use. It is very important to study the originals in order to understand what has happened since Progress overtook him; since the screen and factory dyes fundamentally changed his designs and colours.

We have a great deal to learn from Morris. He made carefully observed drawings and paintings of his garden plants, mastered the intricacies of designing trailing plants, overlapping leaves and blossoms (see Plate 7). He knew his trees, birds and fruits; he sensed the plant's character and growth – all this is evident in his designs. One marvels at the complicated accurate working drawings of his almost hidden repeats which can be seen in the Victoria and Albert, City of Birmingham Art Gallery and Walthamstow museums (see Plate 9). He designed specifically for the block, completely mastering the techniques of cutting and registration. He researched in old herbals and dye manuals and gave his undivided attention to every detail, insisting on the very best cloth and colours. His loathing of those accursed 'Prussian blues' led him to more tireless research into woad and indigo dyeing. He and his dyers built an indigo vat 9ft deep, holding 1,000gal, requiring five dyers to operate it, and 'very pretty it was to see the

1 Indian hand-painted and dyed border pattern c1785–90, resist dyed in madder. The black is 'pencilled' in with iron/tannic, there are three tones of red from alum/madder, purple from iron/madder, yellow from alum and an indigenous plant, and the blue dyed in indigo after waxing. Courtesy of the Olive Matthews Collection at Chertsey, Surrey (*John Knight/West Surrey College of Art and Design*)

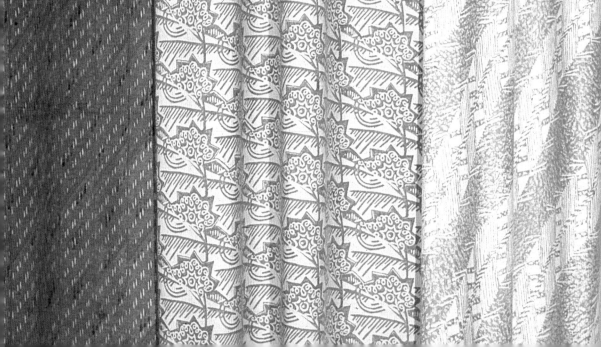

silk coming green out of the vat and gradually turning blue'. His own talent, his own reading and research, his own experiments in design and dyeing – the continuity from first to last – were the essential ingredients for the excellence of Morris's work.

But alas, the inevitable problems of production followed because the work had to be sent out to small factories, and responsibilities delegated. Whilst Morris was in charge, the textiles were of his high standards, of the best available cloth, with the beautiful old dyes, and his very special designs. After his death, cheaper, debased imitations began to appear, 'versions' of his designs were printed by screen with insensitive colour combinations. Go and find some real ones, and see for yourself what they should look like.

I appreciate Morris's enormous talent and have certainly learned a great deal from him, especially from his determination to understand the origins and behaviour of colour and from his sheer mastery of design. For my part I would choose his small scale *Eyebright* print. My personal taste is for simple patterns on the borders of saris, 'popular art' designs on barge doors and handles, fairground horses and stripes on Maltese fishing boats.

The Twenties and Thirties

After William Morris's reforms, artists and craftsmen began to look forward, rather than backward to medievalism as Morris had done. They formed guilds and associations to promote design ideas for a new age, for the machine. These included the Century Guild, founded by Macnamurdo, producing textiles printed in Manchester; the Art

2 Three lengths printed by Barron and Larcher in iron black (*left to right*) *Gordon*, block printed on silk; *Felt Stripe*, printed on linen; *Bunch*, block designed and cut by Dorothy Larcher and printed on silk velvet (*Colin Wilson/Crafts Study Centre, Bath*)

3 Three block prints in iron rust by Barron and Larcher (*left to right*) *Pointed Pip* on cotton velvet; *Mantalini*, on linen, and *Kite* on fine cotton (*Colin Wilson/Crafts Study Centre, Bath*)

Furniture Alliance, formed by Christopher Dresser in 1880, making textiles in London strongly influenced by the prevailing fashion for oriental and Japanese artefacts; C. R. Ashbee's Guild and School of Handicrafts, and the Art Worker's Guild. This last guild led to the formation of the Central School of Art and Crafts, with W. R. Lethaby as head, who believed that students should learn to practise their chosen craft.

All of the above were in some way influenced by Morris's liberating thought, linked with a desire to work for the future, with the machine. Roger Fry, the leading art critic and writer of the time, saw the need to re-establish the artist-craftsman studio, so, together with Vanessa Bell, Duncan Grant, Frederick Etchells and others, he founded the Omega Workshops. They 'sought delight in creation, in the making of objects for common life'. And *they* were going to make them, not the machines. Their work included painted furniture, screens, textiles, pottery, carpets, stained glass and complete interior design schemes, largely influenced by cubist and fauvist trends, resulting in strong, abstract and geometric designs. These workshops preceded those of the twenties and thirties and were of considerable importance to those artist-craftsmen who set up between the two World Wars.

In the early twenties Britain had acres of slums, substandard housing and ribbon development; but the wealthy lived in comfortable country houses equipped with muslin-capped maids, gardeners in baize aprons, a motor car, chauffeur and butler. There were advertisements for 'complete lounge furnishings' from Harrods (one is reminded of the complete kitchens and bathrooms on offer today). Also, mass-produced industrial artefacts became available for suburban semis, detached or country houses, and the printed-textile industry began to invest in screen printing techniques in order to speed up production.

However, several long-established firms continued high-quality block printing, eg, Lazenby Liberty at his printworks at Merton Abbey, which specialised in hand-block-printed silks – many of oriental design. G. P. and J. Baker's firm continued their high-

quality prints, some especially commissioned from artists, others designed in their own studio from Baker's historic archives. In the catalogue of an important exhibition, *From East to West – Textiles from G. P. and J. Baker*, Frances Hinchcliffe wrote:

> The linens were usually block printed. This was a skilled operation, for which the printers served a seven-year apprenticeship. Although this was a slow, and therefore expensive, hand process it did not limit the size of repeats or the number of colours that could be used, unlike the copper roller-printing machines. It was not unusual for up to 150 blocks and thirty colours to be used for one Bakers' design. Most importantly, the particular quality of this careful block-printing gave the designs the liveliness and pleasing appearance of a water-colour wash. Sixty-yard 'pieces' of cloth were printed on slate-topped tables of the same length. Production was speeded up at Bakers' works by having two printers work simultan-eously in the same fabric, one from either side of the table. The blocks were usually made at the printworks. By the late 1940s few new designs were being cut and the last set of blocks was made in 1951.

Plate 10 Block printing at G. P. and J. Baker's in the 1930s. Colour is taken onto the block from a dye pad, or sieve. The woman behind is the tierer, her job is to keep the sieve evenly covered with dyestuff (*G. P. and J. Baker, London*)

Plate 11 *Tropical Fish* designed by Frank Ormrod and block printed in 1939 by G. P. and J. Baker. Underwater scene of seaweed and fish in green, brown, yellow and pinky red, set against a dark-maroon background (*G. P. and J. Baker, London*)

Plate 12 *Quills*, designed by Mea Angerer and block printed in 1934 by G. P. and
J. Baker. Group of three upright feathers, arranged in half-drop repeat, in brown,
white, two shades of pink and a yellow (*G. P. and J. Baker, London*)

C.884

Artists of the time were commissioned to design for industry, and we find the names of Mea Angerer, Gregory Brown, Lucienne Day, Duncan Grant, Ashley Havinden, Christopher Heal, Charles Rennie Mackintosh, Enid Marx, Henry Napper, Paul Nash, Marianne Straub and Alec Walker, among others. Messrs Warner Brothers established their factory on the Darenth river at Dartford in Kent, and produced hand-block-printed cottons, linens, velvets and silks of a very high quality.

The blocks were made by specialist craftsmen from five-ply sycamore wood, and printed with fast dyes on tables of up to 24yd (22m) in length. Warner's range of products included interesting block-printed flags and banners, for which there was a good demand.

Alongside industrial developments there was a burgeoning of the arts and crafts,

Plate 13 Two block prints designed by Paul Nash for *Cresta* silks and printed by G. P. and J. Baker, London, in 1930. C883 consists of two blocks, and the lower one, C884 of four blocks (*G. P. and J. Baker, London*)

leading to the establishment of many outstanding artist-craftsmen. They had to rethink and rediscover for themselves many of the techniques and ideals of earlier years. Nowadays, as a result of phenomenal speeding up of communications, we have a World Craft Council, a British Craft Council, regional craft centres, guilds, exhibition spaces and galleries everywhere, informative magazines, handbooks and directories, and opportunities to work in isolated and faraway places. Help and advice is not difficult to obtain but those pioneers in the twenties and thirties had to find things out for themselves.

Among them, Barron and Larcher were the leading block printers and they had to refer back to eighteenth- and nineteenth-century manuals for their research (see next section). Three or four other blockprinting studios should be mentioned. Enid Marx, a young student from the Central School of Arts and Crafts and the Royal College, joined Barron and Larcher's Hampstead studio in 1925. Her reminiscences of this are printed in the Appendix. After working with them as an apprentice, she set up her own studio, producing block-printed textiles, designs for woven furnishing fabrics, wallpapers, ceramics and plastics for industry. She was and still is a superb wood engraver, having taught the subject at the Ruskin School, Oxford, with Eric Ravilious and Paul Nash in 1931. She produced pattern papers, book jackets and illustrations for children's books written by herself. In collaboration with the Hon Margaret Lambert, Enid Marx collected, wrote books about and arranged exhibitions of, English popular and traditional folk art. It was an exhibition and a book of theirs which supported and enhanced my own appreciation of simple designs on everyday objects. In 1945 Enid Marx was elected Royal Designer for Industry.

In the late twenties Joyce Clissold, a student from the Central School of Art and Design, took over the management of 'Footprints', a block printing studio established earlier by Mrs Eric Kennington at Hammersmith. With Joyce Clissold in charge, it employed thirty assistants in two West End shops (London) and became a flourishing concern making hand-block-printed textiles for both dress and furnishing. Joyce Clissold was a lively and original artist who translated the excitement and fun she found in life into vivacious, rhythmical, often pictorial, textiles. World War II forced the workshop to close, but she continued to draw, paint and make richly textured collages with scraps of silks, velvets, nets and gauzes from her treasury of materials.

Michael O'Connell's work is also relevant as he made large hangings by painting with mineral dyes and using paste-resist techniques. His work was shown at the Festival of Britain; he designed for industry, and made interval curtains for the Royal Shakespeare Company, employing mainly resist, spraying and dyeing techniques with mineral dyes (iron rust) and ICI Caledon dyestuffs.

Karin Warming and Ann Morgan, who trained at Chelsea School of Art in the late thirties, sold their designs to Alistair Morton of Morton Sundour, and were invited by him to work in his design studio in Scotland. Some while later they set up their own block printing workshop near Stowmarket, Suffolk, exhibiting and selling their work in London and through the Artificer's Guild in Cambridge. They used Alizarine (mordant) dyes since the basic and direct dyes then more generally obtainable were not sufficiently fast. The development of the Alizarine dyestuffs called for a steamer and this they built themselves. Sadly, World War II ended their enterprise, and afterwards Karin designed for and sold to industry and taught part-time at Camberwell School of Art. For ten years I joined her there, teaching indigo dyeing and resist patterning in the summer term. It so happened that we had very dry summers during that time, and we used a yard for dyeing and dripping lines.

Barron and Larcher
Phyllis Barron came to textiles by chance, having seen a collection of old French printing blocks whilst studying painting in France. She became intrigued with the blocks, the patterns and their origins, and gradually found herself paying more attention to them than to her painting. Back in London she made enquiries about training, to find someone to teach her the techniques she lacked, but had no luck. However, in the Victoria and Albert and British Museum libraries she found two invaluable works which were to become her *vade mecum: The Philosophy of Permanent Colours* by Dr Bancroft, and *A Practical Handbook of Dyeing and Calico Printing* by William Crookes.

Plate 14 *Basket*, direct print in black (unnamed) on natural linen, Dorothy Larcher's third block (*Crafts Study Centre, Bath*)

Plate 15 A corner of Barron and Larcher's house, 1930. The settee is covered with a linen hand-block print in *Peach* design (*Crafts Study Centre, Bath*)

Barron then began to collect bits of equipment (tubs, basins and cloth) for experimenting in her Hampstead first-floor flat kitchen. She attempted an indigo vat with urine (collected from friends at night), and printed with nitric acid on indigo-dyed cloth to attempt a 'discharge' white pattern. She used a French block which had reminded her of the small flower and geometric designs in indigo-blue and white – the traditional cotton aprons and dresses of the French country people.

Having read Bancroft's description of the uses of iron rust for printing ('It reads like a novel', she said), she found she could buy the ingredients from a firm of dyestuff importers in the docks area of London. There, among other things, she uncovered interesting pieces of old textiles, some used for packing china, spices and tea (see plate 31). Her enthusiasm gathered strength. She followed old recipes for iron black with pyrolignite of iron, powdered oak galls, cutch brown and indigo blue for use with natural linen cloth. These were all then fairly easy to obtain and the results were very beautiful – the colours and cloth having a natural affinity. The colour combinations and quality of cloth seemed exactly right, and a wonderfully refreshing change from the industrial prints then in the shops (see Colour Plates 2, 3 and Plates 17–20). I can do no better than to quote from Robin Tanner's introduction to a memorial exhibition of Barron and Larcher's work held at the Royal West of England Academy, May 1966.

The thirties were their heyday. Production was lavish. Their garden was packed with treasured plants which often inspired fresh designs. Visitors to the workshops were legion. There were frequent exhibitions. It was indeed a rare blend of the feeling and craftsmanship of two people that produced that great wealth of printed cottons, linens, velvets and silks: and although the peculiar contribution of each is clear yet it is not always easy to distinguish the designs of the one from those of the other.

Plate 16 Enid Marx's studio showing printing blocks and a hanging length of white linen printed with black in a design called *Prunes*. Below this is a drawing on paper of a project for Morton Sundour and in the foreground are two lengths of blockprinted linen: (top) *Fish*, a two-colour print; (below) *Butterfly and Cloud*, also in two colours (*Enid Marx*)

43

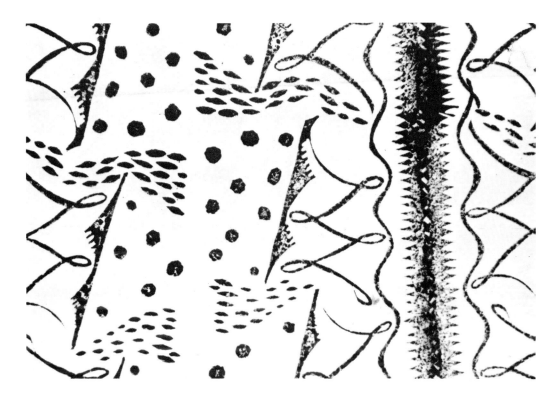

Their work was a revelation at that time and has been a source of wonder ever since; for at its best it has a timeless quality, a peculiar Englishness and rightness exactly fitted for the upholstery, curtains, and clothes for which it was designed. Moreover, the stuffs upon which the blocks were printed and the dyes used were so completely and sensitively understood that there was an inevitability about the work: it was like that because it could not have been done in any other way – there was always a perfect harmony between the fibre, the dye and the block.

Barron showed her work at a few London galleries, including The Three Shields, and the Brook Street Gallery, which in the late twenties and thirties began to offer craft work for sale. She sent also to the Red Rose Guild in Manchester.

Dorothy Larcher had been studying in India with Lady Herringham making records of the Buddhist frescoes in the Ajanta caves. On her return to London she visited the Brook Street Gallery and was charmed with Barron's simple block-printed textiles. They met, and later decided to join up and work

Plate 17 (*opposite*) *Cornucopia*, block printed on linen in brown (*Enid Marx*)
Plate 18 *Loopy*, block cut and printed by Enid Marx (*Crafts Study Centre, Bath*)

together. Their partnership soon flourished and lasted until World War II virtually put an end to their supplies. From the same Brook Street Gallery they were commissioned to print all the furnishings and curtaining for the Duke of Westminster's new yacht – a vast undertaking which necessitated taking on and training help in the printing and making up. Many other important commissions followed and they became well known.

In 1925 they were joined by Enid Marx (see page 40) to work as an apprentice. She willingly helped with the daily workshop chores, which often meant being outside (even in winter), rinsing chalk out of cloth that had been discharged, dye mixing, mordanting, steaming and endless washing. She played a very important part in their experiments and carried on herself later when she set up her own workshop.

Plate 19 *Elizabethan*, 1922, by Barron and Larcher, block printed with iron liquor
on galled natural linen (*Crafts Study Centre, Bath*)

Plate 20 (*opposite*) *Guinea*, Barron and Larcher printed linen c1930
(*Derek Balmer/Crafts Study Centre, Bath*)

In 1928, Muriel Rose (Crafts Officer for the British Council and collector of excellence in craftsmanship) opened her own Little Gallery in Kensington, and held regular exhibitions of Barron and Larcher's work. Through Muriel Rose they found many admiring customers and friends, who kept them very busy.

It became necessary to find other premises, so Barron and Larcher moved to a beautiful Georgian house at Painswick in the Cotswolds. The stables were converted for workshops, an indigo vat was built into the workshop floor, with an overhead pulley and specially made frame to operate the dipping of the cloth in and out of the vat. They experimented with new dyestuffs imported from Europe, and an expanding business developed. One of their greatest joys on leaving London was a garden of very special plants, which provided inspiration of colour, form and texture for many of their designs. Dorothy Larcher was mainly responsible for the block cutting (although of course Barron did some), and Barron was very good at dye mixing and the chemistry involved, due to her study of the old manuals. Girls from the village helped with the printing, taught by Dorothy Larcher. Large commissions were received, eg, curtains for the Senior Common Room at Girton College, Cambridge, and for the choir stalls in Winchester Cathedral.

World War II brought their work to an end: it became impossible to obtain the best-quality raw materials, and marketing was difficult. Dorothy Larcher returned to her flower studies, each one lovingly painted – its character, colour and markings captured in a rare, discreet quality of paint. She completed only about forty of her favourite plants before she died in 1952, leaving Barron to work alone for twelve years after. At times she was sad and dejected, even to the point of considering burning up her store of blocks. In a letter she wrote:

> When we had to stop because of the war it was at first a relief. It had been such a struggle. When things began to slump we sold so little and still had wages and all the expenses going on as well as feeling that people were no longer interested. We had to let the house and camp out in this place which was then a workshop

right through upstairs and the small kitchen downstairs very cold and uncomfortable. For a long time I felt that making anything that looked nice or thinking about it was just a frustration and waste of time. Now I see how unhappy I was and feel I might have done something.

Her loneliness ended and new interests grew after meeting Robin and Heather Tanner. Robin Tanner (HM Inspector of Art) visited Painswick School and called on Phyllis Barron, who was chairman of the school's governors. A long and happy friendship developed leading to her involvement in Robin Tanner's course for art teachers, held annually at Dartington Hall, Devon. At these, Barron gave a remarkable account of her working life, revealing a natural gift for retailing the small and sometimes hilarious episodes such as the occasion when she ran out quickly to get a loaf of bread, forgetting to turn down the gas underneath her indigo vat (a urine one of course), the contents of which she met trickling down the stairs on her return. Barron's contacts with local government, the Gloucestershire Guild and gardening friends kept her very busy, so her later life became happy and fulfilled. I feel extremely privileged to have known her then.

Barron died suddenly in 1964. Her printed and dyed stuffs, including Dorothy Larcher's blocks and paintings, also their collection of antique textiles were passed to Heather and Robin Tanner, Barron having willed, 'Robin will know what to do with them'. For years afterwards, the Tanners patiently sorted, cleaned, researched and catalogued them all. Robin wrote their story in his inimitable hand in two large hand-bound volumes containing actual samples of printed and dyed cloths. These books and an extensive collection of cottons, silks, velvets and linens are now housed in the Crafts Study Centre, Bath.

Two years later, in 1966, the Royal West of England Academy's spring exhibition included eighteen flower studies by Dorothy Larcher. Together with these paintings, a remarkable memorial exhibition of Phyllis Barron's textiles was arranged by Robin and Heather Tanner. It had been many years since their textiles had been shown in public, and there was a very enthusiastic response. In the following year, Barron and Larcher's textiles were shown at the Cheltenham Art Gallery, and were again warmly received and appreciated by textile students, the general public and collectors.

After these two large exhibitions, a group of craftsmen, teachers and others, met (led by the Tanners) to find a way of keeping this work and of making it available somewhere for students and others to see and to study. After more than ten years of negotiation, the Crafts Study Centre Trust was formed and, in the early seventies, a Centre was established at the Holburne of Menstrie Museum, Bath, under the aegis of the Trustees of the Museum and the University of Bath. Its aim is to collect and exhibit the finest examples of work by British artist-craftsmen of the twentieth century. To date, the collection includes calligraphy, ceramics, embroidery, fine printing, hand block printing and dyeing, hand spinning and weaving, metalwork and wood. Examples of these, plus books, workshop and archival material may be studied on request. Exhibitions, talks, discussions and demonstrations are frequently held. Information and enquiries should be addressed to Barley Roscoe, Assistant Keeper, Crafts Study Centre, Holburne of Menstrie Museum, Great Pulteney Street, Bath, tel (0225) 66669.

3 · TRADITIONAL RESIST DYEING

We have considered the ancient colours and the early forms of pattern making by madder dyeing and block printing in India (see Chapter 1), the origins of cotton printing and dyeing in the West. In other countries man thought of different ways of pattern-making through the dyeing process, no doubt as old as the art of dyeing itself. When looking through collections and museums for original examples we find many ingenious ways of 'reserving' or 'resisting' patterns by preventing the dye from penetrating selected areas of cloth prior to the dyeing operations. These included clamping, tying, binding, stitching and knotting. In some other areas, a variety of plastic substances such as clay, flour pastes or wax were used, sometimes in combination with masks or stencils for applying the dye onto cloth.

Our challenge is to find the most appropriate way of expressing an imaginative idea through cloth and dye, as distinct from colour printing. We must always remember that a *method* is neither creative nor uncreative: it is the artist's *mind* that creates.

We know that the art of dyeing flourished in the hot climates where also the best dye plants were found, and to find examples of resist pattern dyeing we should therefore look to some of these countries.

Indian Wax and Tied Resists

Apart from an astonishing mastery of mordant dyeing, India excelled in the use of indigo, especially making intricate patterns. In order to make blue in the madder style it is necessary to cover all parts of a design with wax except those to be dyed blue. These uncovered areas would receive the dye from immersion (of the whole cloth) in indigo, after which the wax had to be removed by boiling off in water. This would give blue flowers, border patterns or leaves, which could then (if so designed) be made green by overdyeing with yellow. This may well have been the earliest form of what we now call wax resist. Having waxed-in all those areas, the designers were only a thought away from using wax on plain undyed cloth to create indigo-blue and white patterns, and this they did.

Red and white, however, presented a problem, since madder must be developed in a heated vat which would melt the wax. Another solution was found: possibly because someone noticed a white mark appearing where a holding line had been tied to lift cloth out of a dyebath. This led to the idea of tying in small stones, beads, etc, prior to dyeing. Indian women artists grew their finger nails especially long and pointed to help them pick up the tiny portions of cloth; then their exceptionally nimble fingers tied it up into incredibly small knots.

Another feat was to make striped patterns for turban cloths. There is an enormous range of these, their designs bearing significance to tribe and trade. In Colour Plate 5, you see a bright-yellow and black turban cloth partly bound into a long snake, and partly untied. The cloth is a fine muslin, 2–3yd (2–3m) long. It would have been dampened and stretched diagonally between two workers each taking an opposite corner and skilfully twisting the cloth into a long

4 *Ogee* print from hand-engraved wood block by Enid Marx, 1930s. Black and tan on linen (*Colin Wilson/Crafts Study Centre, Bath*)

5 Turban cloth from India, source unknown. 2-3yd (2-3m) fine muslin, tied and bound, dyed black over gold. Partly untied to reveal the stripes (*Ski Harrison*)

skein, binding it around in pre-determined stripes. You can see this clearly in the photograph. For checks, these bands would be untied, re-bound and re-dyed in the opposite direction.

There are many examples of tied-and-bound cottons and muslins to be found in museums, also now in Indian import shops, though over-exposure is limiting their appeal. However, it is to be hoped that the best will be preserved. If you can, look at a collection of variously patterned early Indian textiles: painted and printed calicos, band-hanas, shawls, muslin saris, turban cloths, preferably together with Indian paintings and music. You will sense the superb mastery of the textile arts and the skills in colour dyeing, which are so delicately expressed in Indian miniature paintings.

African Pattern-Dyed Indigo (*Adire*)

Unlike India, Indonesia and the Far East, there is little evidence in Africa of a traditional use of wax as a resist, though there is a long history of indigo pattern-dyeing. There are those who affirm that indigo dyeing originated in Africa, where there is an abundance of wild plants including *Longchocarpus*, *Ficus* and *Jatropha* containing the blue colouring matter indigo, along with evidence of ancient 'blue' settlements and dye pits around the villages. There are surviving examples of old ceremonial and religious blue and white patterns, variously made by resist methods, continuing through to the twentieth century. Sadly, however, returning travellers report that it is becoming increasingly difficult to find good pattern-dyed indigos (*Adire*) in today's markets. The country has become westernised and appears bent on forgetting the old craft traditions.

There are two publications of great

6 *Adire* indigo-dyed cloth from Nigeria, exceptionally tightly oversewn in a diamond pattern. (*left*) The cloth unstitched but unwashed; (*right*) dyed cloth before unstitching showing fine oversewing (*Ski Harrison*)

7 Linen tablecloth. Double-painted paste-resist in olive-green, tan and ivory, using Soledon dyes. Courtesy of Deryn O'Connor (*Author*)

interest on *Adire* methods of resist. They are No 54 of *Nigeria* magazine, and a small book, *Adire Cloth in Nigeria*, edited by Jane Barbour and Doig Simmonds. The latter gives first-hand accounts of *Adire* dyeing methods, the origin of some of the designs and an essay on the chemistry and general history of indigo dyeing (see Bibliography).

The most famous centres for indigo pattern-dyeing are in Abeocuta and Ibadan in Western Nigeria and in Kano in the North (see Colour Plate 6). Indigo blue has remained the favourite colour and it is patterned in many ways to make clothing and other cloths for domestic and ceremonial uses. Cloth is worn simply wrapped around the body, and displays to the best advantage the strength and beauty of bold indigo-and-white designs. Some of the work is undertaken by men, but most of the processes were carried out traditionally by women.

The early, and now very rare and sought after, *Adire* were patterned and dyed on handspun, handwoven cloth. This was superseded by imported Manchester cotton which is used for most of the *Adire* found today. The basic process used was tying – exceptionally cleverly done by ladies (like the Indian ones) who grew their finger nails specially long (see Plate 21).

Stitching in its various forms, ie, over-stitching, gathering, pleating and later machine stitching, produced yet different effects. The material would be folded, rolled, or pleated, stitched and bound. In Senegal, West Africa, elaborate *embroidery* designs were stitched prior to indigo dyeing, and later un-stitched (see Plates 23-5).

Some of the most famous symbolic, pictorial examples were made by yet another method, that of painting on a layer of starch which, when dry, acts as a resist to the indigo dye. The starch, which is painted on by women, is extracted from their tropical cassava plant (a variety of tapioca) and is boiled with alum and copper sulphate to their own special recipe. This solution hardens on the cloth, in the sun, and prevents the penetration of indigo dye. After dyeing, which is the men's province, the gluey starch is removed, leaving a white pattern on a blue ground.

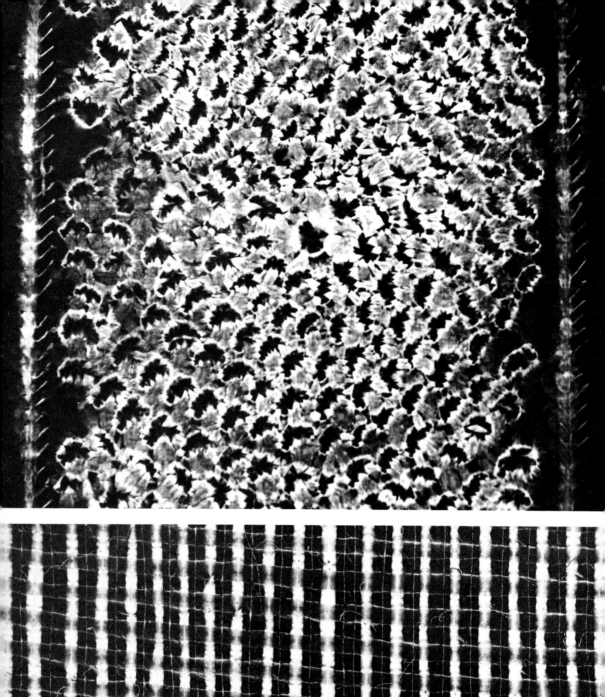

Plates 23, 24 Patterns made by embroidering white cloth prior to dyeing in indigo. After the stitches are removed, the pattern appears white on a blue background. From Senegal, West Africa (*Museum of Mankind, London*)

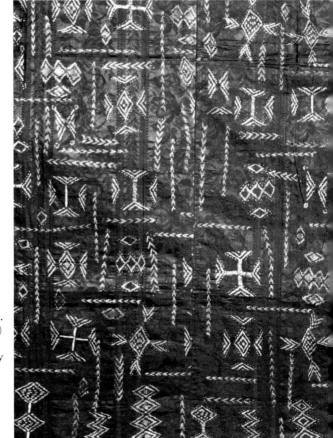

Plate 21 (*opposite*) *Adire* cloth from Abeocuta. Tied, stitched and dyed in indigo (*Stephen Hoare*)

Plate 22 *Adire* cloth folded and overstitched by machine, from Abeocuta (*Stephen Hoare*)

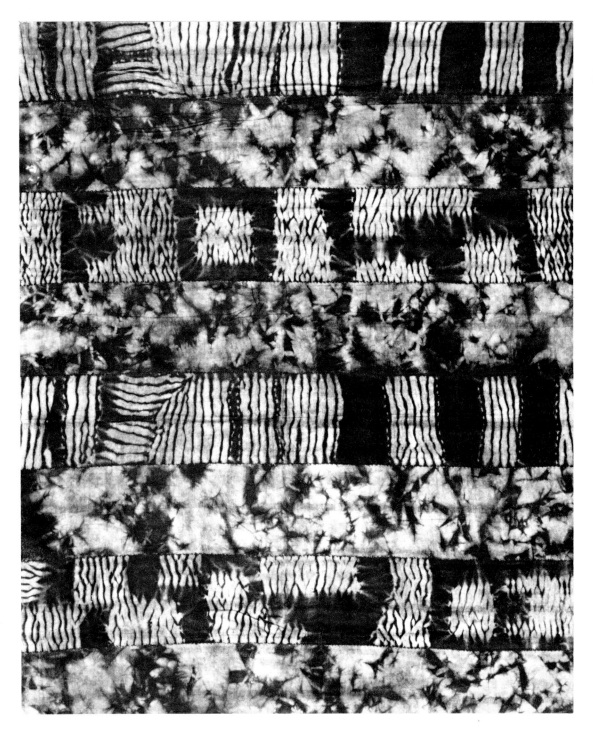

Plate 25 Strips of Senegalese tied and stitched designs sewn together
(*Museum of Mankind, London*)

Plate 26 (*opposite*) *Adire* cloth in traditional designs painted with cassava flour paste
by women and young girls. After drying the paste and dyeing in indigo the paste is
removed, leaving white patterns on a blue background (*Stephen Baker*)

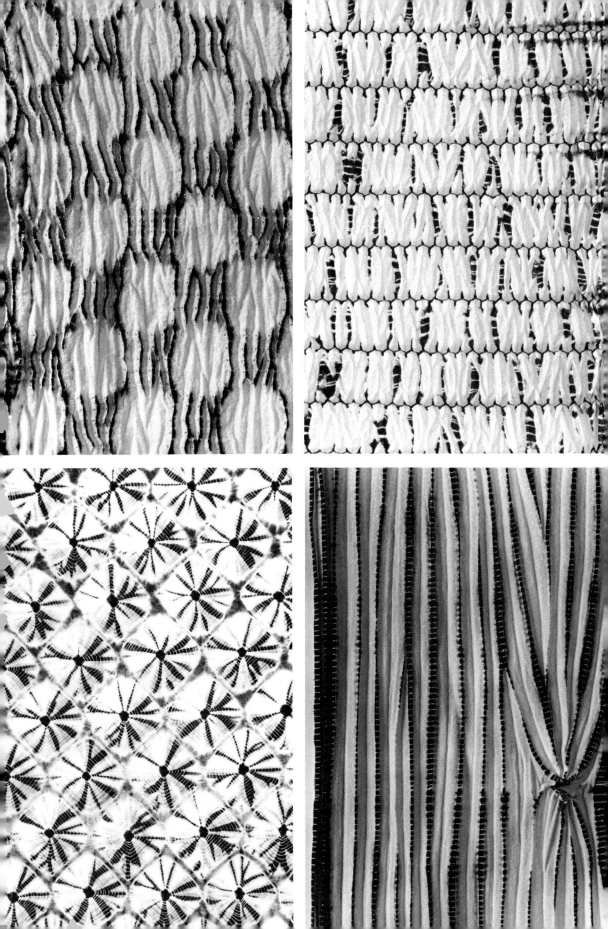

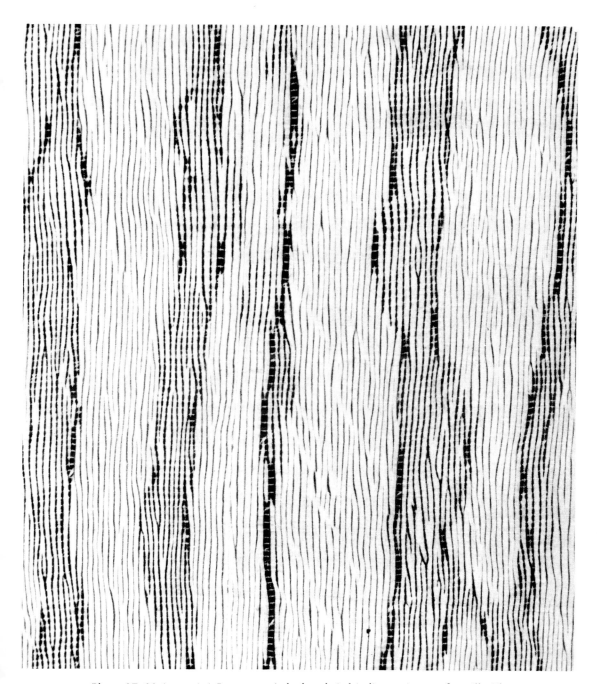

Plates 27–30 (*opposite*) Japanese stitched and tied indigo resists on fine silk. The needle marks are visible, showing clearly in Plate 27 how the final pattern appears after dyeing in indigo. Plate 28 shows fine stitching on a tuck, and binding in between these rows. Plate 29 has patterns of neatly tied circles and 30 is pleated lengthwise down the cloth and bound tightly (*Ethnological Museum, Basle, Switzerland*)

Plate 31 (*above*) Japanese fine cotton, which was bound and tied into a long snake, then dyed (see turban cloth in Colour Plate 5). This was found by Phyllis Barron packed around a tin of dyestuff from the East. The fineness of the pleating and binding is exceptional (*Stephen Hoare*)

Japanese Shibori and Katagami

The textile arts of Japan, particularly those of dyeing and resist techniques, are rightly famous, and one needs volumes to record the painstaking precision and achievement of Japanese craftsmen and women. We find old texts and early woodcuts of Japanese craftsmen at work which confirm that their mastery of resist dyeing techniques was as near complete as is humanly possible. These exceptionally gifted craftspeople are respected and honoured today as 'Living Treasures' (see *The Living Treasures of Japan* by Barbara Curtis Adachi, Bibliography).

The Japanese excel in the spinning and weaving arts, and from early times they produced wonderfully fine cottons and silks which were decorated in a variety of ways. Japanese herbalists and medicine men discovered ranges of lovely colours – most importantly indigo, which is very nearly Japan's national colour for everyday working clothes. We will look at examples of two important methods; *shibori* which covers a large range of sewing, binding and tying processes; and *katagami*, stencil cutting for use in paste-resist dyeing.

Not being able to visit Tokyo, Kyoto or Nano, I visited one of the best collections in western Europe, housed in the Ethnological Museum, Basle, where (in a storehouse) there are beautiful examples of Japanese *shibori* on fine silks and cottons. An article in *Time* magazine (1976) reported that:

> Only one craftsman could work on the length of cloth since even a change of workman – or even a brief illness – could result in an irreparable alteration of the rhythm of the tying and the evenness of the results. The knots took more than a year to tie and another to undo, one by one. Because the process costs so much, the making of them was outlawed by the Japanese sumptuary laws of 1683, which attempted to control extravagance in clothing.

One would not advocate a repeal of those laws, but still must gasp in admiration at this work, which can inspire modern achievements – more suitable to our civilisation.

The technique of flour-paste resist has been used in the East for many centuries. The

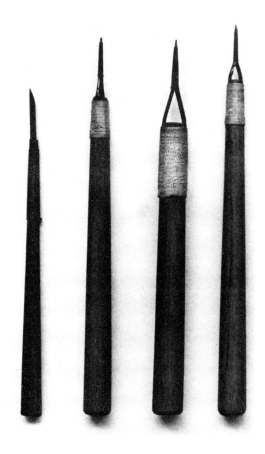

Plate 32 Japanese stencil cutting tools (*Stephen Baker*)

8 (*opposite*) Paste-resist stripes, twice dyed in iron rust on linen by Annette Morel. Also, a length of tied resist (with half grains of rice) by Heather Williams on cambric, dyed in iron grey by the author (*Stephen Baker*)

9 (*overleaf*) Length of painted paste-resist stripes on poplin, overdyed in Soledon blue; with an iron-rust print of triangles, pasted and overdyed in rust (*Jonathon Bosley*)

10 (*overleaf*) Block print in Soledon red tan and double wax-spot resist dyed in Caledon reds (*Courtesy Marjory Mewton*); twice-dyed fine calico in iron rust, patterned by double rows of tucking (*Jonathon Bosley*)

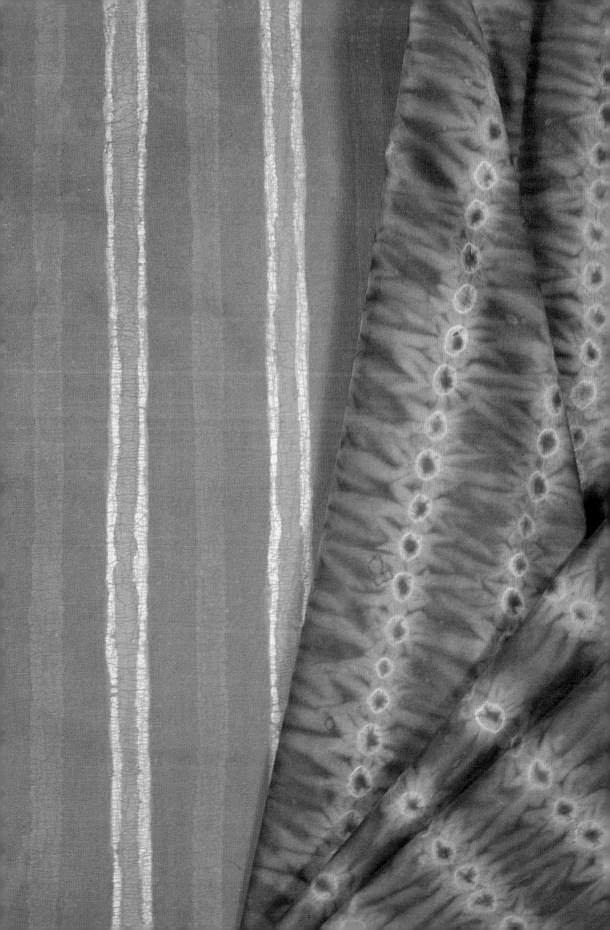

11 (*left*) Tablecloth in double paste-resist stripes of blue and tan on percale. In foreground, *France 82*, a triple block print in blue and tannish red on high-quality Swiss satin-striped poplin (*Muzz Murray*)

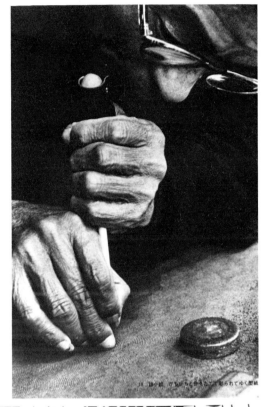

Plate 33 (*right*) Japanese stencil cutter at work (*Stephen Baker*)

Plate 34 (*below*) Stencil of carp swimming among weeds – a favourite Japanese subject. From *Japanese Stencil Designs* Dover (1967), a republication of the original c1892 (*Stephen Baker*)

paste was originally laid on by a stick, hand-made tool or brush, and later on, the use of blocks, stencils and screens was developed. China and Japan have a variety of flours, eg rice, lime and soya, plus trees and shrubs in abundance as raw material for their famous paper. It is not difficult to imagine, therefore, that the Chinese and Japanese have become masters at stencil making and cutting. Plate 32 shows some Japanese stencil cutting tools, and Plate 33 shows a stencil cutter at work. (The carp diving about in swirls of weeds is a favourite theme.)

The stencils are traditionally cut in pairs from very strong thin paper: one is laid flat and covered with adhesive, over which (a feat of accuracy) a net (or single strands) of fine silk or hair is laid. The second stencil is then placed in position, so perfectly that the separate layers cannot be detected. The fine hair lines (visible in the picture) keep in position rings and other complete shapes which otherwise would fall loose. Background patterns are often spotted, made by piercing the stencil with sharp knives.

Japanese pastes for use with stencils are specially made from rice flour and rice bran to the craftsman's preferred consistency. They are coaxed through the stencil with a spatula. After drying, the cloth is dyed in indigo. From the carp stencil (Plate 34), a white fish swimming in blue waters would result, the reverse of the stencil. These methods are widely used to decorate working clothes, bedcovers, children's pinafores, wraps, etc. The Chinese designs show freedom and gaiety, whereas the Japanese are more sophisticated and stylised.

Wax Resist

Further south and east, in Indonesia, there is a long and famous tradition of using wax as a resist to make richly patterned *batik* cloths. Those from Java are generally accepted as the finest examples, though some other islands, including Sumatra, have practised the technique. It is thought that the process found its way east from India, where very early on wax was used as a resist to make chintzes, as we have seen. The wax was probably originally laid on with a stick, the ends possibly chewed and frayed to form a brush. Later, with copper and its craftsmen at their disposal, the Indonesians invented a convenient little tool called a *tjanting* (see Plate 44). This tiny 'saucepan' holds the hot wax and keeps it hot, whilst it trickles down the small spout to be drawn on the cloth. The spouts vary in size and number according to the design requirements and the worker's skill.

Study, if you can (if only from books) the magnificent grandeur of Javanese traditional architecture, sculpture, shadow puppets, dancer's costumes, and court head-dresses, and listen to their gamelin music. Batikking was considered a suitable pastime for the ladies of the court and aristocracy, as was embroidery in the West. Plate 35 shows one of the most famous traditional designs, the Princely Pattern *Parang Rusak*, originally reserved for royalty and its court entourage. Plate 36 shows two Javanese lady batikkers: notice the wooden frames for holding the cloth. Such a frame is comfortable and convenient to handle and to move the cloth forwards and backwards whilst waxing – it helps the batikker to see where she is going, and ensures that the wax settles in the cloth. If the cloth were placed on a backing sheet, the wax would tend to penetrate and settle on it. Notice the charcoal stoves, pans of hot wax, the box of tools and inevitable cups of tea with lids.

Later on, following the tradition of *tjanting* painting, and in order to speed up production, a copper block was invented for printing. This was called a *tjap* and was made by specialist copper craftsmen. It was also operated by men, whereas women used the *tjanting*. It is the women's products, drawn by hand, that remain the most valuable and eagerly sought after. The *tjap* produced small repeating patterns that have a charm and character of their own, very different from the flowing drawn lines of the wax pen.

Plate 35 Traditional Javanese design, the *Parang Rusak*, drawn with *tjanting* and wax and dyed in indigo and brown (from a tree dye) on a cream background (*Victoria and Albert Museum, London*)

Plate 36 (*opposite*) Javanese lady batikkers, from Stutterheim's *A Pictorial History of Civilization in Java* (*Stephen Baker*)

Plate 37 Detail of silk shoulder cloth from Palembang, South Sumatra. Stitch and tied resists followed by overprinting. (*Tropenmuseum, Amsterdam, collection no 1698-1723*)

Plate 38 (*above*) Poncho garment of bark cloth, pattern-dyed by clamping resist process. Author's collection (*Stephen Hoare*)

The introduction of modern dyestuffs in a wide range of colours, and the popularity of wax painting as a craft, have influenced a new movement to both East and West batik painting. This involves the creation of both pictorial and abstract pictures and wall-hangings. I use wax only as a simple resist for small spot or diaper patterns on a dyed ground, and to 'light' up a block print, like a star in a dark sky.

Clamping Block Resists

Plate 38 shows one of the earliest garments dyed by an equally primitive form of resist. The 'shirt' is of bark cloth, and the design is made by folding and pressing the cloth between two blocks. The origins and details of this one are unknown, but the fold marks are plainly visible. A dye or stain from boiled-up leaves would have provided the light-brown colour. Bark cloth is made from the inner bark of mulberry and fig varieties growing in tropical countries. The inner layers would be peeled off, in some cases boiled up, followed by lengthy beating, which finally provides a strong paper-like cloth. (There is a certain tree in South America called the shirt tree, whose bark can be peeled off to provide an almost ready-to-wear shirt.)

This folding and clamping method was developed and used in the East (particularly in Japan) on a workshop scale, using clamping, pressing boards which were intricately cut with mirror-image designs. The cloth was placed in-between the twin boards, clamped or pressed together to prevent dye from penetrating those parts in relief. When immersed in a colour vat, the background became dyed and the clamped-together images remained the original colour of the cloth. For further reference and illustrations, see CIBA Review 1967/4.

69

Plates 39 & 40 Slovak printer at work using wood block and kaolin paste resist. From *L'Imprimé indigo dans l'Art Populaire Slovaque Prague* (1954) (*Stephen Baker*)

bleaching liquor has passed through, a stream of water is made to follow to clear the bleaching liquor . . . the result is a pattern of white spots upon the red ground.

This method was adapted in the nineteenth century in Scotland for the manufacture of bandhanna handkerchiefs, those with patterns of white spots on a turkey-red ground. The method was described by William Crookes in *Dyeing and Tissue-Printing*:

This style, intended for handkerchiefs, is generally a distinct business apart from ordinary calico printing. Leaden plates are used, perforated with holes of the exact size, shape, and distances of the spots. A pile of handkerchief pieces is laid between two of these plates, so that the holes exactly correspond and the whole is then subjected to several hundred tons of pressure, specially modified for the purpose. A solution of bleaching liquor (chloride of lime) is then allowed to flow through the holes . . . and percolate downwards . . . as soon as the

Wood-Block Printing with Resists
Other adaptations from ancient methods were adopted in the nineteenth century, especially paste resist which was used in wood-block printing. Three very different examples are shown here. Plates 39 and 40 show a Slovak printer in the nineteenth century using a block printing resist-paste for indigo. The block would have been hand-cut in relief by a specialist craftsman, and it represents a typical peasant-style design of the eighteenth and nineteenth centuries. The paste was made from kaolin, gum arabic, lead acetate, lead sulphate, copper sulphate, oil and alum. The proportions would vary according to the printer's preference, and would be made especially for him. The photograph clearly shows the use of a 'tiering tray' (see Chapter 2), the careful

Plate 41 Resist print for indigo. Woodblock printed on linen/cotton with a different
design on each side. French 1760–1790 (*Royal Ontario Museum, Toronto*)

placing of the block's registration point, and the way the printer is working down the length of cloth. As the cloth became dry, it would be raised and hung over poles beside the print table, thus avoiding the cost of (and the space needed for) a very long table. Depending on the design, I often use this method of hanging lengths over bamboo poles. They are then out of the way and can dry slowly – a very satisfactory method.

The example in Plate 41 is of a resist print for indigo, wood-block printed with a different design on each side. This interesting method was used quite extensively in Europe, and this example was made in France, about 1760–90.

The third example, in Plate 42 shows the hem of a dress (1815–20) in the Devonshire Collection of Period Costume, Totnes, Devon. The design consists of two different forms of printing. A block print of paste formed the diagonal, curving stripes, by resisting the blue indigo dye. After this dyeing operation, the cloth was overprinted with a 'milled' roller. The resist pastes at that time were compositions of metal sulphates, oils and alum, which were discontinued after the invention of aniline dyestuffs.

In Chapter 7 there are adaptations of paste resists made in my workshop, and see also Colour Plates 7, 8, 9 and 17.

Plate 42 Hem of a dress (1815–20) in indigo blue, chocolate brown and white. The diagonal stripes are wood block-printed with a resist paste prior to indigo dyeing. The overprint is from a milled copper roller in chocolate brown, made by printing madder on alum and iron mordanted cloth. From the Devonshire Collection of Period Costume, Totnes, Devon (*John Knight/West Surrey College of Art and Design, Farnham*)

4 · THE WORKSHOP, EQUIPMENT AND MATERIALS

Water

If you look at the contents page of old dyeing and printing manuals, you will notice water high on the list, if not at the top. The selection of water for dye and print works used to be of prime consideration, and this is why they were situated near selected streams and rivers. Of course, over the years, these factories played a considerable part in polluting the neighbourhood. The great cost of setting up a print works in the country away from the town's effluent was of secondary importance to a good clean water supply. In 1785 James Napier wrote:

> It would be a great object for the dyer to obtain pure water; or, if this is not practicable, to know what the ingredients are that are in the water he is using, so that he may either counteract their effects and escape their consequences, or render them subservient to his purpose. The great practical importance of water to the dyer is not only its neutrality but also its solvent power. The cohesion of solid bodies is overcome, and the particles are diffused through those of the water, and so placed in the best possible condition for combining with articles of other bodies brought into proximity with them.

So it was, and, very early on, trouble arose between factories because effluent from the black dyers upset cleansing operations farther downstream; or, as in southern France, the acid deposits from the Avignon madderers caused serious pollution. This situation has worsened to danger point today and one can seldom, if ever, find clear river water.

William Partridge, an eminent dyer in the early nineteenth century, said, 'The impediments in the way of our dyers consist in the variableness of the water, the itinerancy of the dyers and for want of the goods dyed being properly cleansed.' The old dyers insisted that if the water was too hard for washing (and curdled soap), it was not fit for dyeing. It also could not be too soft; the important quality was consistency, so that adjustments could be made.

Nowadays, water is rarely found in its natural state. Mains and town water are treated with strong cleansers and in some places recycled, so it is a chemist's job to adjust the water to the dyestuff. Water softeners are available (eg Calgon) and good dyebooks contain instructions relating to their use. You have to make your own adjustments for preparing cloth, scouring, washing off and dye mixing. If you have access to real wild water you are very lucky. You could test the difference in using that and the mains supply, and see for yourself.

Dyeing and printing use water for the scouring and preparation of cloth, washing-off after dyeing, and final soap washings and rinsings. Therefore, we must plan for sinks and taps in convenient places and make sure, if at all possible, that we have a sensible outlet for effluent.

For my workshop here at Sigford, the supply of water comes from moorland springs, and we are very careful with it. We store rainwater both for the garden and workshop. The sinks are placed facing an area where an adequate soak-away has been dug, and into this go all the used dye vats and other undesirable liquids. Obviously, this is not always possible, but it should be considered where practicable.

The planning of living and working areas always requires thought, and the more experience the better. Kitchens and art/craft workshops are particularly tricky, as you often do not know in advance where the most convenient place for that sink, plug, light, stove, shelf should be. It is all too often after you have started to work that you feel you must change. You need to make imaginery tracks around the available space and imagine you are actually doing the job you are planning for.

Workshop at Adult Education Centre, Dartington

In the 1960s at Dartington, Devon, a group of textile enthusiasts were given the unique opportunity to set up a dyehouse and print-room at the Adult Education Centre. In co-operation with the Dartington Trustees and Devon County Council we were able to open the dyeing and printing course for several days per week. In this way, members were able to come in between shopping and housework or for longer periods, and to learn the essential continuity of thought and attention necessary to any craft.

The dyehouse was specially planned, and housed in a pre-fabricated classroom unit. Starting off with an empty rectangle gave us a one-and-only chance to plan equipment, cupboards, tools, dye vats, plumbing, sinks, stoves, dripping lines and tables – just where we thought our passage of work demanded. We imagined entering the room with an armful or basketful of prepared cloth (in all probability wet) for the job of dyeing. Where do we put this down, where are the mixing bowls and spoons for dye-making, where are the recipes, vats, gas rings and sinks?

We followed the processes through and were able to plan a wonderful dyeing paradise. We already had a large and well-windowed classroom with store cupboards, tables and sinks with hot and cold water. This room was planned as a 'clean room' where designing, paper work, ironing, and clean washing took place. It is always important to keep these activities well away from dyeing which is a very splashy business. The vat dyeing kitchen was positioned at right angles to this room in order to make a soakaway, and this gave us a narrow connecting area (known as the Polish corridor), where there was space for a 2-3yd (2-3m) print table, cupboards and a worktop suitable for dye-measuring and mixing.

Inside the vat room, a concrete gully was built on two sides for hanging dyed cloth wet from the vats. One side was designated solely for indigo, the second for other colours. Gas rings were positioned at a conveniently low level, some sinks were high, others were low – for filling and emptying buckets. Worktops were covered in formica; there were shelves everywhere and tables in the centre.

Serious interest was created: students and staff from other colleges came to work. We studied textile history, and experts visited to lecture, and show examples and films. There were painting and drawing courses, ceramics, sculpture, the allied crafts of spinning, dyeing and weaving, plus basket-making, hook rugging with dyed materials, paper making, visits to museums and galleries, all in collaboration with the Dartington College of Arts. Looking back, it was a unique educational experience which certainly enriched and influenced my own work.

Sigford Workshop

In 1966 we moved to a smaller house, with more land and a range of farm buildings. Four loose boxes in a Victorian stable block were converted into my workshop. This was a very much smaller space than that at Dartington, but the knowledge gained from its planning and use was extremely helpful: clean areas, dye gullies and hanging space were priorities. The adjoining shippon provides, when needed, additional hanging lines and storage, but the workshop (approximately 50sq m – 540sq ft) is quite large enough to heat during the winter. In the warmer months, one can work outside with dye vats, hanging lines, tables, etc – and life is quite different.

A stove, be it an Aga, Rayburn or woodburner seems to me essential. It will heat the room and the water, cook the dyes, air damp cloths and boil a kettle for tea. The Rayburn (secondhand) and washing machine (early model for preference) are concentrated on one side, with the plumbing, facing the farmyard area. There are two sets of double sinks; one set near the Rayburn is for hot and cold water, the other set, with mangle, has only cold water. These are low-level sinks for filling and emptying buckets and vats; they all drain into the soakaway.

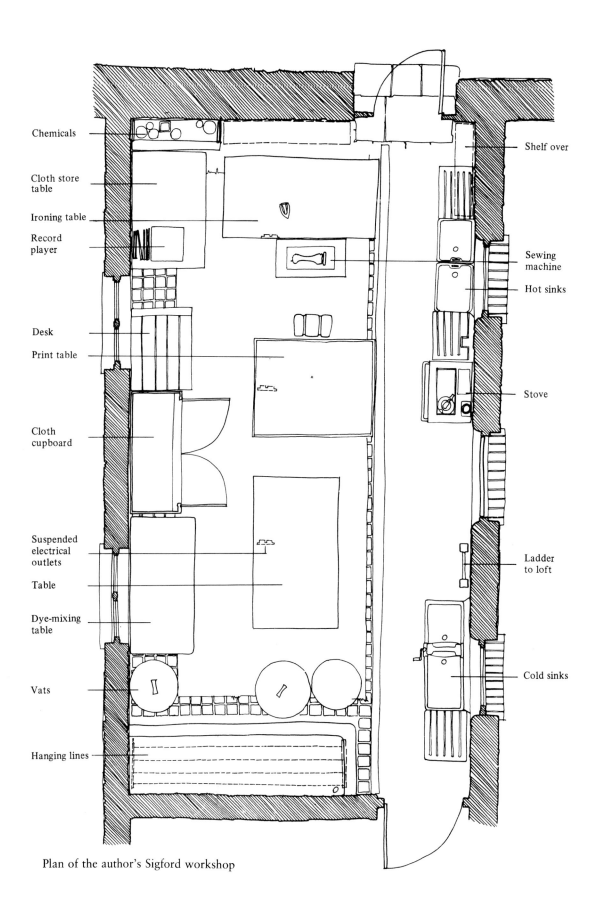

Chemicals

Cloth store
table

Ironing table

Record
player

Desk

Print table

Cloth
cupboard

Suspended
electrical
outlets

Table

Dye-mixing
table

Vats

Hanging lines

Shelf over

Sewing
machine

Hot sinks

Stove

Ladder
to loft

Cold sinks

Plan of the author's Sigford workshop

Along one end is a dye gully, with drainage and hanging lines above. This is an essential – you need a ditch to catch surplus dye and drips. You can place the vats in front of it and, as you lift the wet cloth out of the vat, the hanging lines are right there for pegging out. To complete this job perfectly, all you need is a third arm to take one end of the cloth and hold it out flat, whilst with the other two you cope with the pegging! Lines and hanging space wherever you can place them are extremely convenient for hanging clean or freshly printed stuffs up and out of the way. Clean areas, storage for new material, and a large cupboard for printed cloths should be placed away from sinks and dyes.

We all have to confess our earnings and spendings, so a desk and shelves are needed for trying to keep accounts and stock-books, patterns, files, drawings and all the paper work. Then there is the ironing area and a print table, with convenient lighting. There are always changes to make and never enough time to work out all one wants to do. Everyone's workshops will be different, so there is little need to explain every detail, but in printing and dyeing the most important considerations are: to keep clean and tidy, to separate wet operations from dry clean ones, to ensure a safe electric circuit (think of all the wet processes), good plumbing, sink exits and a soakaway.

The plan of your workshop will be influenced by what you do, of course. It was only after beginning to work again at Sigford, teaching almost full-time for a number of years, that I realised the extent of textile disciplines I had become involved in. Barron and Larcher were printers, superb artist printers. They used Swiss and German dyestuffs and the old iron/tannic black and indigo, but always for print methods. I had become seduced by indigo resist dyeing; tying up tiny spots, away from the workshop, out in the sun or beside the fire. Waxing and paste resisting are equally enjoyable and a change from block printing, which can be tiring. Also, and this is quite important, it seems right to have a choice of printing and dyeing processes going on simultaneously, so that no time is wasted waiting for cloth to dry before fixing, or for a vat to mature. There is always something ready for your attention and the life of the workshop is continuous – which is as it should be. Notwithstanding, it has made the arrangement of my workshop very complicated and sometimes difficult to operate, as tools and equipment are needed for block-making, block printing and its related dyestuffs, three resist methods and their appropriate dyestuffs. In addition, I need space for the preparation and storage of cloth.

I have assumed that you are not starting completely from scratch, ie, waking up one morning, deciding to be a block printer and/or dyer, making a list of materials and tools, and forthwith setting up. You will have had experience, either on college courses or in industry; or you have a serious interest in doing it yourself, and have already collected some tools to experiment with. An exhaustive list of tools is, therefore, unnecessary, but you will need some kind of workbench for making blocks, an assortment of well seasoned wood (preferably fruit wood), plus saws, glue, cutters, gravers, knives, measuring tools and storage facilities near this bench. The most obvious and useful tools and equipment for each process are discussed below.

Block Printing Table

Starting off with only the money I could 'pinch' from housekeeping, most of my equipment was bought in markets and house sales, and in the fifties there was a wonderful supply of real bargains. We used to buy pine tables (strong kitchen ones) for a pound or two, scrape off the paint and find handsome wood underneath. For the print table we found three odd tables and combined them into one. The legs and supporting frame began life in Rattery village Post Office: the top was worn and there was a slot in it through which money was passed into the drawer below, but the legs were extremely sturdy. Stretchers from a second table reinforced the top, and the third table, from someone's mahogany dining room suite, was as flat as a billiard table. Two legs were missing but this didn't matter as the top fitted quite well over the Post Office frame.

Plate 43 Author in her Sigford workshop (*Richard Davies/Crafts Council*)

This top was fixed down, covered with four layers of grey army blanket and topped with a thick waterproof cover (stretched and bordered with 1×1in wooden strips). Thirty years later, this combination table is still in use.

Tiering Tray or Dye Pad

Barron and Larcher used tiering trays and gave me an old one to experiment with. However, there just wasn't room for it, either on the table, or on a trolley beside it, so another solution had to be found.

Altogether I wasn't very happy about the tray. Look at the photograph of the man resist-paste printing on page 70. The paste is spread on taut material stretched over a frame which floats on a bath of gum made stiff. But what if this (stretched) material begins to sag? Imagine you are picking up dyestuff with a block: I realised that dye would easily creep up the sides of the cut surfaces and settle where it was not intended. This meant cleaning the block each time before printing. It seemed to me that a convex surface would help to prevent this. I had also seen a similar gadget at David Evans and Co (block printers at Crayford until the late 1970s). We therefore experimented with wooden blocks covered with a slightly convex surface, then waterproof cloth. Over this cloth was fixed a felt or blanket, on which the dyestuff was evenly spread.

The choice of felt or blanket and the way in which the dye is spread are among the most important skills in learning to print evenly. This method also enabled me, when making blocks for my linear designs, to choose a longer length than would conveniently work on a tiering tray. This is easier to demonstrate than to explain. What one is trying to do is to spread dye evenly over the cut surface of a block, and it seemed sensible to make a slightly curved pad on a wooden base and to have several sizes of these to fit the blocks: some are small and square, some long and rectangular.

The covering material which holds the dye should be chosen according to the mark you wish to make on the cloth. A textured cloth (ie blanket) could give a slightly textured print; a fine calico would not hold as much dye as felt but might prove exactly right for printing small spots. One has to experiment, keep an assortment of dye-pad cloths and make tests for each block before printing. What are you trying to express? This mark should be as sensitive as any made by a painter with a brush. Between your hand and the cloth there is just the block charged with colour.

The dye should be of exactly the right consistency and should be spread evenly over the dye pad. This rhythmical skill is one that comes with practice and experience, and gives great pleasure when the time and motion is exactly right. These remarks perhaps belong to Chapter 6, but they are mentioned here to illustrate the choice and use of a dye pad.

Block-Printing Hammer and Other Tools

A block printer's tools and equipment should include a block-printing hammer. These are specially designed with a heavy lead head, short wooden handle with a rubber ferrulled base (see Plate 44). The block is tapped with the rubber end, not the metal. Other items include:

long metal rule (1.25m or 48in)
large set square
tape measures
tailor's chalks
dark-coloured Sylko
yoghurt pots
strong glue (Bostik clear), suitable for
    sticking linoleum to wood; cork and
    plastic to wooden block backings
1-3in (3-8cm) brushes (a good selection)
mixing bowls (plastic is suitable)
set of spoons
wire whisk (for dye mixing)
scalpel knives
cutters and gravers (see page 80)
thermometers

Blockmaking

In the cotton-printing industry, a separate shop was allocated to blockmaking. There, a master-craftsman would cut blocks from specially seasoned fruit woods (or sometimes

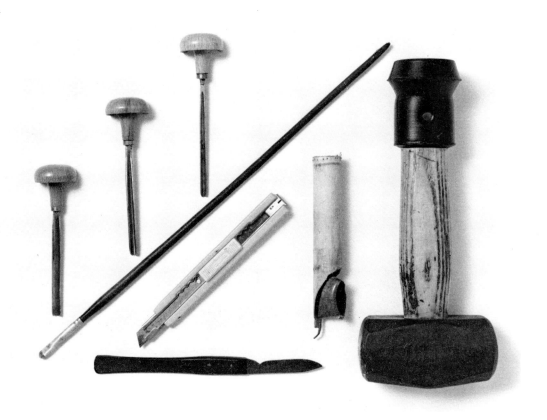

Plate 44 Tools: cutters, barbered brush for paste resist, *tjanting* (second from right) and printing hammer (*Jonathon Bosley*)

'pin' the designs on with small metal pins), following designs sent to him from the design department of his firm. An individual's workshop is different: you must design your own patterns, and cut, or otherwise fashion, them from whatever substances give the desired impression on cloth. I have used wood, linoleum, cork, loofah, rubber, fine plastic foam and other substances. You need to collect seasoned wood blocks for cutting or for sticking linoleum, etc, onto.

Linoleum

Linoleum, invented in 1860 by Frederick Walton as a waterproof floor covering, is made from ground-up cork, resins and other fillers, combined with oxidized linseed oil, and finished with a waterproof surface. It was not invented for block printing and no-one seems to know who first thought of cutting into it for a printing block. Perhaps the memories of unskilled prints for school Christmas cards have cast a shadow over its respectability as a suitable print medium.

12 (*opposite, from left*) Triple-block print in Soledon dark brown and a yellowy/greenish brown on cambric. Iron-rust block print, wax resisted and overdyed in indigo, with the printing block below. Twice-dyed rust on strong cotton, overprinted with two blocks in dark olive-green and tan. Courtesy of the Crafts Study Centre, Bath (*Jonathon Bosley*)

13 (*overleaf, from top*) Dress length in dark olive green with indigo-blue circles, which were printed first, then resisted with wax and overdyed in green. Soledon and Caledon dyes. *HH* two-block print in tan and dark blue on grey-poplin dyed ground (*Stephen Baker*)

14 (*overleaf, right*) Double block-print in blue and tan on satin-striped crêpe cotton, made into a blouse by Maura Leighton. Dark-blue printed stripe on brown-dyed poplin, tucked (*Stephen Baker*)

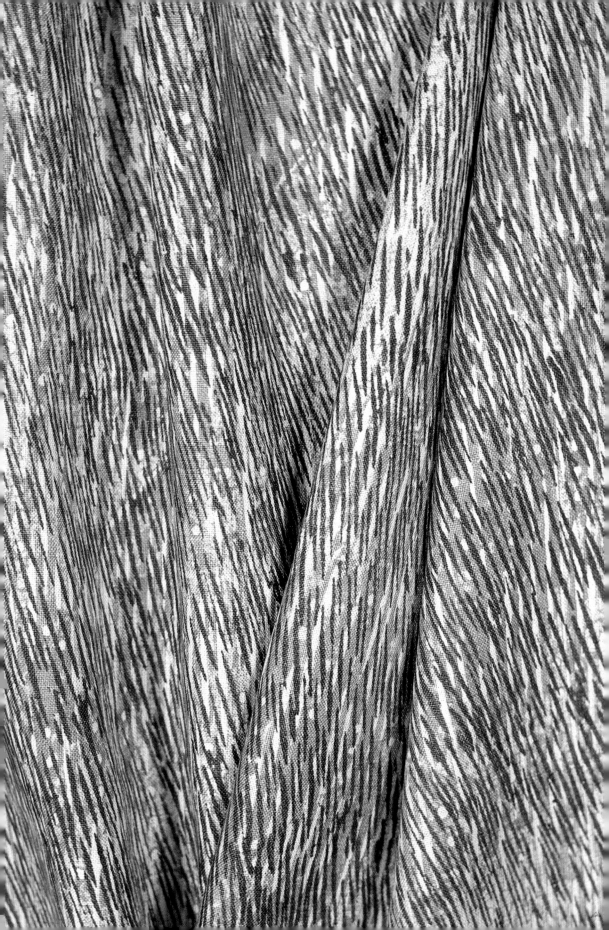

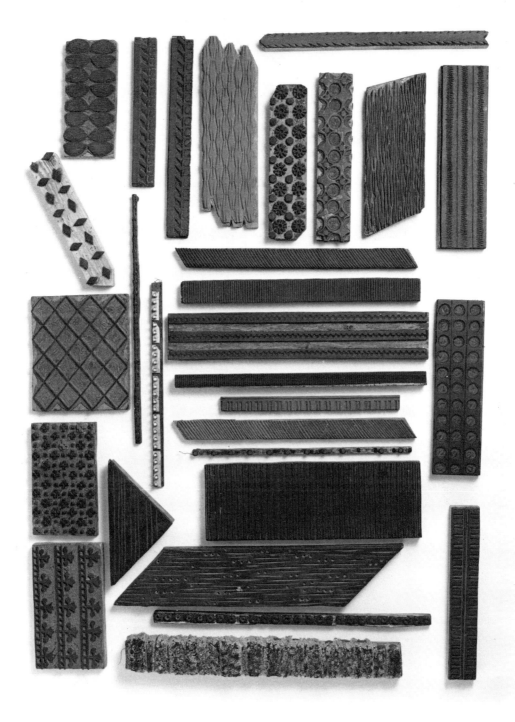

Plate 45 Blocks made by the author (*Jonathon Bosley*)

15 Two-block print on heavy Irish linen for Dartington Hall study curtains, in grass-green and brownish black. Courtesy of Crafts Study Centre, Bath (*Stephen Baker*)

However, well-established artists have used linoleum with great success, and it certainly possesses advantages over other substances like wood and metal when textile designers are learning how to cut. After all, the final effect depends on how it is cut and used. Lovely, simple prints have been made with the humble potato and parsnip.

Barron and Larcher were highly skilled with linoleum and their blocks of the twenties and thirties look as though they will last forever. They 'drew' with cutters and knife, expertly controlled, transforming into pattern the decorative qualities of garden flowers, and rhythmical abstract designs. Their blocks can be studied along with the great collection of their textiles at the Crafts Study Centre, Bath.

The best kind of linoleum for block cutting used to be known as 'battleship'. It was a mid-brown colour, quite thick and an excellent fine consistency that did not break up under knifing and graving (addresses in Appendix IV).

One last point: linoleum has a waterproof surface which does not readily accept dye-stuff, but it does however give quite an interesting textured effect. In order to make the surface more absorbent and thus print more evenly the surface should be sand-papered. It is easier to cut if warmed but beware of overheating it, in which case there is a danger of it crumbling.

Dyestuffs

Space must be found to store dyestuffs and dangerous chemicals, eg, caustic soda, sulphuric acid (for developing Soledons) and an assortment of other acids and minerals. Printing dyestuffs are very expensive and are usually in extremely fine powder form; so fine that some almost invisible particles may float about (especially if there is a draught) and settle on clean material. Ideally, dye measuring and mixing should be in a place apart. If this is not possible, then care must be taken to cover clean areas whilst the measuring and mixing is going on.

Accurate balance scales are needed, and kitchen scales will do for some purposes. You will need dozens of clean containers for mixing colours; plastic bowls (preferably with lids), mixing spoons, brushes, and various sizes of dustbins and plastic troughs, depending on the dye methods you decide to use. Look in industrial catalogues for strong plastic bins and troughs – some garden shops stock useful shapes and sizes. One cannot plan all this in advance; you find out as you go along. It is surprising what useful objects and odd machines you can find in second-hand shops and markets. Look out for enamel bowls (free of cracks), enamel sauce-pans for heating dyestuffs, galvanised wash tubs (without blemishes), plastic buckets, an old-fashioned rubber mangle (exceedingly useful for testing samples and small amounts of cloth). Save up for stainless steel. In fact, you need a glorified kitchen, as dyeing is very similar to cooking.

The ingredients and equipment for indigo dyeing should be kept separately, and this process should ideally take place apart from everything else. The indigo dyeing procedure is described in Chapter 8.

Choosing and Buying Cloth

Hand printing and cotton materials associate well, but, for the best results, you must look for top-quality cloth. Cotton has been, and still is, of great economic importance the world over. The cotton plant (*gossypium*) is a member of the *Malvaceae* (mallow) family, and several herbaceous and shrubby varieties from hot and semi-tropical regions provide good-quality fibres. The best are: Sea Island from *Gossypium barbadense*; Egyptian and American Upland from *G. herborium*; and, from India and China, *G. arboreum*.

When the cotton boll is ripe, downy fluff (lint) forms around the seed heads and must be picked as soon as possible, then graded into lengths of staple. The best cloths feel soft and silky, yet firm and smooth, and have a lively appearance. Poor-quality stuff looks drab, creases easily and dyes a miserably sad colour. Sea Island or Egyptian cotton is a pleasure to work with, improves with wear and washing, feels both crisp and silky and irons beautifully. Stevens' *Fabricopedia* says that, 'Typewriter ribbon is the tightest fabric in the world and only Egyptian or Sea Island cotton is used to make it, in high thread counts of up to 320 per square inch.' There is no one place where stocks of all kinds are kept. One hundred per cent cotton (pure wool and silk also) is becoming difficult to obtain, as a great deal is now mixed with man-made fibres. Keep a file of suppliers and samples.

Before the introduction of the metric system, cloth was roughly divided into *furnishing* fabric of 48in width, and *dress* fabric of 36in. At the present time, you can still find these in some shops and markets, alongside ranges of 1m and larger metric widths, suitable for soft furnishing and dress. Shop around and make the necessary adjustments. As a general rule, furnishing fabrics are wider and heavier than dress, but often a dress fabric can be used satisfactorily for furnishing, and vice versa. In the days before central heating, furnishing cloths tended to be thick and strong, with possibly lighter versions for the summer months, but nowadays they are generally lighter. If you are designing for curtains and covers, it is important to plan your design to repeat exactly selvedge to selvedge, so that wider widths can be joined accurately.

An assortment of cloth should be kept in stock, and preferably related to design methods, eg, block printing, waxing, pasteing or tie-dyeing. This may involve a good deal of searching in shops and markets, buying offcuts, etc. Try to keep in mind what you are buying the cloth for – those lengths to be dyed in indigo, that order for bedroom curtains or strong calico aprons, a range of fine cottons for the next exhibition, or cambric for small tying-up patterns. It is a good idea, before putting the cloths away, to label each with its type and length, date and place of purchase, and the purpose for which it was bought.

Plate 46 Wringing a length of indigo-dyed cloth (*Richard Davies/Crafts Council*)

Backing sheets

These are made of fairly strong calico (bleached or unbleached) or sheeting. They are pasted down on the waterproof print-table covering to take up dye which may penetrate the cloth being printed, and also to assist in marking registration guide lines. Several are needed, since they need to be boiled after each printing session to remove traces of dye. The sheets should be hemmed to prevent fraying.

Washing and Ironing

Double sinks for washing and rinsing are invaluable, also a constant supply of hot water. Printed and dyed textile operations include many wet processes, in fact the workshop often looks more like a laundry than a textile studio.

Ideally, two washing machines are convenient; an automatic for putting cloths through a programmed wash, plus an old-fashioned one. This latter should be one which you can stop and start when you want to see what is happening; one that will just do a boil, or a spin, or a half load – for which an automatic programme is unsuitable. The earlier machines are more versatile, more akin to hand-washing first in hot and then in cold to find the effect of colour on a sample. Look for a good second-hand reliable model, and have it checked by an electrician before use (and regularly serviced).

I use a bio-degradable cleaning powder 'Ecover' for the machines. It is a cleansing agent that contains no phosphates, no chemical or optical bleach. If this is unobtainable, use good-quality soap flakes.

Again, two irons are useful: one good steam model for perfectly clean fresh cloth and final presentation; the other for sampling and testing colours, ironing dyed papers and any other jobs during which an iron may be tainted. Sprays are useful, as irons seem never to hold sufficient water for lengths of cloth. If at all possible, keep the ironing table for *ironing only*.

A first-aid box should be kept visible and regularly checked.

WARNING

The art of dyeing, as explained in this book, is a form of chemistry and involves the use of 'chemicals' in one form or another: some are more dangerous than others. We are very aware of the dangers and have planned the workshop effluent to fall into a deep underground pit. The amounts I use are, however, comparatively harmless, in fact much less harmful than most of the household and garden sprays and highly toxic insecticides freely available in shops today. We are members of the Soil Association, and have kept an organic garden and farmland free from chemical fertilisers for forty years.

If, however, you wish to experiment, as I have done, for interest (or educational purposes), *please* be very careful and sensible with the dye recipes and ingredients. Take precautions: a mask to prevent inhaling strong solutions, careful ventilation, and protective clothing and gloves.

---

5 · PATTERNMAKING AND DESIGNING

Patterns come from everywhere; from shadows, from scrubbing wood, from writing, from birds in flight, from cooking and raking, from scraps of paper and bits of metal, houses, rain, wind on the sand. Everywhere and everything. The mind's eye – if it has been trained to look, to see what is in fact just there – will help one to remember the stream trickling over the weir steps, the dark ripples, the trout's spotted back and tail as it flicks through water as fast as an electric current. It will also tell you when to stop looking and relate something of what you have seen to clay, textile, stone, wood, knitting, whatever it is you are working with. One cannot explain a design, how to do it; there is no one formula. You see, you think, you work at it, you put things together, you draw, take them away; moods come and go, ideas go round and round until something channels them into an answer – and away you go. Added to this, is the indefinable skill acquired through hard experience and, simply, the love of working with the chosen materials.

There are volumes on design and concordances of pattern; on the theories, philosophy, symmetry, geometry; the religious and symbolic meanings and influences; signs and symbols which we have devised to decorate houses, boats, clothing, utensils, the body and furniture. Perhaps in the first place, they were simply to mark this from that, holy from wicked, yours from mine; or perhaps they were done just for the intrinsic satisfaction and pleasure of pattern-making and designing. Where, in this complicated area, do we begin? As with planning materials and tools, there is no starting from scratch. One must have worked at possible designs and exercised the mind's eye to register images of colour, form and texture.

A musician told me that he might be supposed to think of and perhaps comment on his work in two main ways. Firstly (and most importantly), he would be aware of a certain pattern of sounds which excited, interested and haunted him, and this might have come from any of the influences on him of previous composers or natural or man-made sounds – just something in the whole world of sound which he is aware of, and, being a musically sensitive person, he would probably hear it being played by an oboe, or sung by a soprano, or whatever. The point is, he would not necessarily know its origin, but it would be some pattern of sound from his past experience. Thus, it is into personal experience that we must look to begin to appreciate what is commonly called 'inspiration'.

Secondly, the musician would tend to think of any work more technically, in that at any given time he is likely to be particularly interested in certain chord sequences, methods of development, type of composition, etc, and he would treat his theme accordingly. Obviously, there is scope for interaction between these two approaches to the work of composition. In the same way, patterns and designs come from many sources, and link in the imagination with colours and textures.

We will consider three main categories: linear, floral and geometric; in association with the most appropriate choice of cloth, colour and method of execution. However excellent the design, cloth can be ruined by poor workmanship, and vice versa.

Linear Patterns
Suppose one is interested in lines; seen in fields of sprouting crops, on railways and motorways, on blinds, animals and birds, shadows of fencing, or whatever. Designs of plain stripes can be very elegant and satis-

fying if the method of patterning is appropriate, eg, repeating a plain line with a block may not be right, as the joins are very difficult to mask. This is why some of the most satisfactory linear designs are made by the roller printing machine, which prints a continuous line from an engraved roller automatically charged with dye as it rotates. Linear prints by block can be interesting if the 'join' is intentionally designed, eg, with a small motif. However, this introduces an additional ingredient and the solution depends on what one is attempting to express.

For my part, I am happy to work in a resist method, eg, paste, stitch or wax, to produce lines whose character and texture evolve from the way they are made. See Colour Plates 7, 8, 9, 11, 14, 16 and 17, which show linear designs in paste, sewn and tied resists, overprinted with a 'broken' or designed line. Think of the satisfaction of simple woven stripes, especially the grandeur and harmony in Navajo Indian blankets; some are strong, energetic and exuberant, others are serenely simple. They were woven on an upright loom, and sometimes hung on the house door, rather like we would hang a painting. We have a great deal to learn from these designs, to enrich our study of lines – their proportions, their suitability to the width and length of cloth, the use of colour in relation to background, the choice of print or resist methods. Stripes move and change direction as they are worn (or hung). The Navajos knew how to wear such cloths and wove their chief's blanket (see Plate 47) wider in warp than in length, so that the powerful stripes would lie across the chief's shoulders and arms. Imagine the impact of strong indigo, near-black and white stripes on a dark man against that vast arid landscape.

In your nearest natural history museum, look at the prodigious variety of stripes (and

Plate 47 (*below*) Navajo chief's blanket (*Museum of Mankind, London*)

Plate 48 (*opposite*) *Jagged stripe*, block printed on unbleached calico and dyed in Soledon brown by the author (*John Knight*)

spots) on, for example, insects; weevils, bark beetles, moths, bugs, caterpillars and mayflies. Look at the fine lines on shells, which clearly follow growth patterns in fan or spiral form. We learn about the delicate quality of these lines, the soft but firm texture of the shell, and its opalescent colour. To translate this into a printed textile, you would have to search out an extremely high-quality Swiss cambric, or fine percale, and make a very pale, cream dye for the background. A pattern of lines (perhaps with a spot) would need to be carefully, delicately printed. After all, stripes have a natural structural relationship following the course of warp and weft. Colour Plate 7 shows an example of crossed stripes. The sequence of work is to paste thin lines weft-wise, dye in dark-tan Soledon dye, fix and wash off paste, dry, then paste wider, vertical stripes and when dry dye with Soledon olive-green. Finally fix, remove paste, wash and finish. This results in a lively vibrant brown with the olive and tan stripes crossing. The simplicity of this pattern discloses the subtleties of the veining in the paste technique. Colour Plate 18 clearly shows the different effects from paste-resisted lines (in the foreground) and machine sewn lines, alternating with a small tied spot. Lines appear in some form or another in the majority of my designs – they seem right.

Floral Patterns

Lines and stripes need careful planning for colour and proportion, but a much more complicated design problem is presented by interpretations of flowers, leaves and whole plants. One should certainly look again, with a fresh eye, at the painted and dyed chintzes. The early ones were drawn directly onto cloth with no repeating forms – the 'pen' and brush were wonderfully controlled, the stems, leaves and florets making a delicately trailing design (see Plate 49 and Colour Plate 1). Even though the painter was restricted to madder and its mordants and indigo, the colours were complementary and satisfying. The painter had passed the stage of drawing flowers and leaves as he first saw them, and was indulging in abstractions, developed

from his intimate knowledge and observation.

Suppose we follow his example, and study the real thing. First of all, we have to find 'real' subjects, not in pots in florists' windows! We need to find habitats where plants are growing naturally – uncultivated land, woods, streams and rocks where flowers, weeds, ferns, bushes and trees are indigenous. Look at the trees. Every one is different and has its own form – different in winter from in summer. What about its bark? Is it smooth, is it glistening white and papery like the birch? Is it striped like the snake-bark maple? Does it have horizontal morse-code dashes and dots like the grey poplar? Underneath in the shade are tiny fragile plants with thin soft stems and pale leaves; plus strong thick-stemmed chaps with leathery leaves, ground hugging species spreading their branches flat and creeping in between stones, and others with climbing habits supported by neighbours. Some heads look upwards, some droop and others wait for the evening darkness before opening. All this of course becomes hard to find as modern life encroaches on our wild environment.

The next best thing may be to look at early herbals and plant studies. The print and drawing departments of museums will have them. While you are there, look also at the botanical drawings in natural history museums, at shell collections, stones, geological formations, birds and feathers, as these complement the plants' environment. Illustrations for the Elizabethan herbals were made directly from nature, and referred to as 'living figures', since they portrayed details of flowers, leaves and root systems to enable the herbalist to identify them for his remedies. The artists often fashioned their drawings into an ornamental square or rectangular shape, a style admired by William Morris and his associates, who adapted it for their own decorative work.

16 Two-block print in dark-blue and brown Soledon dye on cambric, courtesy of Crafts Study Centre, Bath. Child's jacket in fine muslin, printed in Soledon blue and brown by the author, quilted with flannel lining, and made by Paula Morel (*Stephen Baker*)

Plate 49 Hem of dress, c1813–18, French or English. Fine cotton, block printed and painted using madder and probably Prussian-blue and weld. From the Devonshire Collection of Period Costume, Totnes (*John Knight*)

17 (*opposite*) Stripes of small white circles, printed with permanganate/citric discharge on indigo-dyed calico, followed by manganous chloride overprint. Courtesy of Marjory Atkey (*Stephen Baker*)

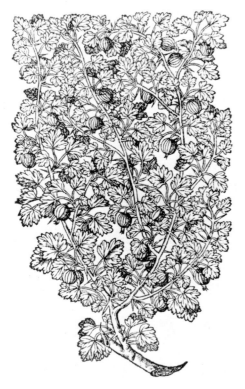

Plate 50 Gooseberries from *Gerard's Herbal* c1143 (*Stephen Baker*)

For a book cover, Burne Jones took the wind-flower and white-lily drawings straight from Gerard's sixteenth-century herbal.

Later, in the eighteenth century, artists were engaged to draw and paint flowers for decorative and scientific purposes. Among them, the work of Georg Ehret (1708–70) is outstanding. He drew with a sureness of touch, accurate vision and a sympathy and sensitivity to the plant's growth and form, displaying a talent for compromising between the artist's and the scientist's approach. An excellent book, *The Art of Botanical Illustration*, by Wilfrid Blunt (see Bibliography), enlarges on the fascinating history of plant painting and painters. His first quotation, from Ruskin, is, 'If you can paint one leaf you can paint the world.'

Look also at the flower paintings of the great artists; Chinese brush drawings, Cézanne's geraniums, Hockney's rose, Dürer's grasses, Balet's dianthus in a milk bottle, his star-like weeds. Think of Monet's love of flowers, his beautiful garden, his paintings of it and the use he made in his house of colours from them. We see the exquisite delicacy of feeling in Dürer's work, Fantin-Latour's roses tell you all, Redon's field poppies are different from Bonnard's, and we are in real wild places when we look at Robin Tanner's water avens, dead nettle, henbane and speedwell.

Studies, then, of real flowers and of the multitude of ways of depicting them used by artists in a variety of media will help and stimulate pattern-making and design. During this period, the mind's eye should be reeling with ideas recorded in drawings, paintings, photographs, and words or phrases which help to clarify intentions. I prefer to experiment, quite early on, with dyes and cloth and to make marks with a small block before planning a large one.

Block cutting and printing are discussed in the following chapter: here, we are considering the bones of pattern-making. To help with this, and with organising repeats, there are two useful reference books; *Pattern and Design* by Lewis F. Day, and *The Grammar of Ornament* by Owen Jones (see Bibliography). There are dozens of others, but the basic common sense and good illustrated examples in these two are worth a study. You will find explicit diagrams of many repeat methods. Practising with these, using a very simple single motif, will stimulate and demonstrate pattern and design rhythms, and build up a tremendously useful repertoire of possibilities.

If your ideas do not lend themselves to print methods, then make small samples of tied, waxed or pasted effects, always keeping in mind what it is you want to express. It is important to remember that what can be done on a small sample cannot always be repeated on a large one. This must be borne in mind and allowed for.

There are free 'painterly' patterns, without exact repeats, made for specific purposes (eg, scarves, wall hangings, etc), but here we are

Plate 51 *Evenlode* working drawing by William Morris, 1883 (*Victoria and Albert Museum, London*)

97

considering repeats which should fit between the width (ie the selvedges) and have a proportionately good repeat lengthwise.

We can therefore think of the cloth as divided into repeating squares or triangles or meandering lines, as a basis for florals or other types. Look at Plate 51, showing Morris's *Evenlode* chintz. The cloth is divided into rectangles and meandering lines, over which stems and flowers are drawn at regular, repeating intervals. You will find a series of such basic grids illustrated and described in Lewis Day's book, eg, the feather pattern, the ogee, the wave, the scale, the diagonal stripe formed upon the basis of a diamond. Morris and his colleagues used these for their chintzes, tapestries, carpets and hangings. They were of course in use long before their time and occur in the earliest manuscripts, embroideries, carpets, etc.

Geometric

These basic grids obviously make patterns themselves, and we can think of squares, rectangles, diamonds, triangles, circles and waving lines as elements of design. They are found in patchwork quilts. Look at the diamonds organised into the American 'sunburst' quilts, the amazing variety of patterns over patterns evolving from eg, the 'Log Cabin' arrangement. These are full of inspiration for block printing patterns and colours. There is no end to designs from crossing lines, circles, half circles, triangles and squares. To make them interesting we must find the right combination, proportion, colour, texture and choice of cloth.

The iron-rust print in Colour Plate 9 is an example of a simple geometric form developed into a richer pattern. The basis is an alternate line of triangles, printed in rust with a potato block (a potato because its

surface is strangely willing to pick up the mineral dye and make an even, flat and sharp-edged print). The rust dye is then fixed and washed. This is followed by painting on paste lines following the stripes, masking half the triangles. Over this, is brushed a coat of iron-rust dye. After fixation, and removal of the paste, a richly veined texture and double iron stripe is formed.

Another source of bewitching designs is *Order in Space* by Keith Critchlow (see Bibliography). Block printers need not worry if they do not understand the geometry of a 'rhomic triacontrahedron', or a 'truncated icosidodecahedron'; their visual shapes and interlocking qualities are fascinating, interlocking and covering space in an orderly and repeatable fashion. They link with the geometry of Islamic pattern, ably described in *The Language of Pattern* by Albarn, Smith, Steele and Walker.

These constructions and grids help us to interpret our imaginative ideas into a repeating pattern on cloth, bearing in mind the importance of an appropriate choice of cloth, dye and method.

Sometimes of course everything falls magically into place. After endless trials, colours seem exactly right, the design links clearly with remembered images, but it doesn't link directly with any special grid or formation – there is no explanation of why it all seems just right. You can't turn it on, or press a button to make it happen. There is just a marvellous feeling of relief that it is right, of a frenzy which prevents you from attending to anything else until you have captured all the information and qualities safely onto cloth, into pattern and colour. But I think we have to endure all the preparatory exercises, trouble, study and agony before the relief.

6 · A PRINTING SESSION

There should be a fair stock of cloth in the cupboard from which to choose lengths for various jobs, but you must also ensure that it is fit for dyeing.

In print factories, cloth for the printworks was delivered in what was called its 'loom' state directly from the weavers, and its preparation for printing sometimes took as many as nine processes. It went first of all to the 'grey room' where all unbleached goods were stored and examined for faulty weaving, dirt, damages and other defects. It was marked accordingly; its quality, origins and date of arrival recorded, to trace faults and make comparisons with other deliveries. Apart from grease and dirt from the weaving shed, cotton contains about 5 per cent of natural impurities that are more or less insoluble in water but can be removed with alkalis and acids. Unbleached calico often has fine hairs and filaments on its surface, and these, which would obviously impair printing, had to be removed with a 'singeing' machine.

Scouring and Bleaching

In order to remove the impurities insoluble in water, cloth should be boiled in an alkali, and in earlier times this was a 'lime boil' followed by scouring in sulphuric acid. Two or more repetitions of the process were sometimes necessary to clean the cloth. After the last acid bath, the goods were washed in bleaching liquid, then well rinsed and dried.

The older method of bleaching, used before the introduction of bleaching agents, was called 'grassing' or 'crofting'. Cotton and linen cloths were laid out on grass fields after scouring with alkalis and acids, and exposed to the joint action of light, air and moisture. In dry weather the cloths were sprinkled with water. The effect of grassing is considered to be due to the action of ozone

and peroxide of hydrogen which are usually found in small quantities near the ground. I can remember tea towels and pillow cases being laid out on the lawn 'to bleach' during a sunny day and overnight, especially if a frost was expected.

Nowadays, calicos and cottons are not generally available in 'loom' or 'grey' states, for which fairly drastic cleansing operations are necessary. However, most cottons contain some form of dressing and this must be removed before printing and dyeing, as the substances used for dressing might well be detrimental to dye fixation. The following is a good cleansing recipe.

Put the cloth to soak overnight in cold water. If in the morning this is very dirty, wring out and repeat the process. Then boil up for about 30 minutes in sodium carbonate (washing soda) at 50g per litre (8oz per gal). Rinse well, wash and dry.

Should you discover that the quantity of white cotton you have bought does not require cleaning off, do not assume that your next batch will be the same. You may be told that it is the same cloth, but it is not worth taking a chance. Cleanse as usual, and test. In any case, an extra boil in soda followed by rinsings helps to make the cloth more absorbent to dyestuffs. Dressings and other foreign bodies in cloth are often the cause of poor dye penetration and loss of colour during washing-off after dyeing.

Remember that these preparatory scourings, washings and rinsings tend to shrink the cloth. Some cloths will shrink more than others, so it is wise to take tests, and make allowances when matching sizes of prints and lengths to be printed.

Mercerising

You may find some cottons are 'mercerised', and that they accept dye very readily. The process was discovered in 1844 by John Mercer, who noticed the effects of caustic alkalis on cotton fibres. He was trying to filter strong caustic soda solution through cotton cambric. It passed very slowly and, at the same time, the cloth became semi-transparent, contracted both in' length and breadth, and thickened. After he had removed the soda by washings and rinsings, he found that the stuffs had gained in weight and strength, and possessed an increased affinity for dyestuffs. His discovery was followed by a patented mercerising machine, but it was not then generally adopted because of the enormous loss of cloth by shrinkage. However, later on, Thomas and Prevost discovered that if the mercerising took place under tension, to prevent the shrinkage, it gave a silky lustre to the cloth, which remained during and after the dyeing operations. These then are the lustrous cottons and poplins that we can now buy. They do not normally contain dressings, but nevertheless it is a good rule to give them preparatory washings.

It is possible to approximate the mercerising process, but not under tension, by using the following recipe.

Add 5g sodium carbonate (washing soda) per litre of water ($\frac{3}{4}$oz per gal) and boil for 30 minutes. Add 150g sodium hydroxide (caustic soda) per litre ($1\frac{1}{2}$lb per gal) and boil for 15 minutes. Rinse well, wash and dry. ALWAYS PUT CAUSTIC SODA TO WATER; NEVER POUR WATER ON CAUSTIC SODA.

Preparations for Printing

As with many other jobs, the preparation takes longer than the job itself, and one never starts from zero. Art cannot be taken out of a cupboard, used, and put back again until next time. Cloth has been bought, prepared for use and packed away; tools and equipment should be in place; and work in several stages is ready to be carried on to the next stage. The following is an example of a session in my own workshop, showing the development of an idea and the processes involved.

Suppose a waxing session has just finished, leaving the table free for printing, and

suppose, whilst waxing those small spots, I have decided which design to work on next. It is to be the three-block brown-and-white print in Colour Plate 12, where I have used an image I know well, and have worked out possible interpretations using three blocks. It comes from the time in May/June when the beech and oak buds are beginning to open in yellowy, greenish brown; their reflections in the river flicker and change colour. Spring rains have darkened the tree branches and barks – they are almost black, and make rippling shadowy stripes in the water. A pictorial representation of the trees, river bank, rocks, water and reflections is not possible for me. I see it transformed into a pattern, but, of course, in the hands of an expert engraver of the eighteenth century, in the style of the Toiles de Jouy, or Nantes, a charming landscape tableau could be displayed over the length of cloth.

Working drawings and notes have already been made, and at this stage I always long for two pairs of hands – one to make up the dyestuffs and the other the blocks – so that when the blocks are ready to be tested the dye is immediately available. However, there are pauses in the mixing up of dyestuffs, and one can usually manage to do a bit of each job as one goes along.

The dyestuffs to be used are the Soledons, for which the recipes are given in Chapter 7. For the wet barks, a strong brown 3RS recipe was used with the addition of a little of the dark blue – to take away the warmth from the brown as it is supplied. Two yellow-browns are mixed, one slightly yellower than the other. Two dye pads are needed; one for each colour. Their size and the covering pads will be chosen after the blocks are made.

It is difficult to decide how much dye to make up, and, since dyes and their ingredients are very expensive, I plan to use up the prepared quantities. However, I always make up slightly more than I think I need, as it is impossible to match the original colour. Soledon dyes keep for several weeks so there is always a chance to print smaller pieces.

Blockmaking

Three blocks are needed, and linoleum seems

best for the lighter horizontal lines. To give a speckled effect I do not sandpaper off the waterproof surface. The lines are cut into it with a favourite scalpel.

I know there are 'lino tools' and manuals on 'lino-block printing' but one doesn't *have* to use lino-cutters and gravers. Try them out, certainly, but if they do not give you the printed effect you are striving for, try something else. After all, one can cut lino with a kitchen knife, a chisel, or any bit of sharp metal. You can burn it out, cut it with scissors or file it down. It all depends on what you want to express. Think of a golfer and his bag of 'tools', his irons and woods and putters to help him hit a small ball for short or long distances, to manoeuvre it out of a ditch, and to coax it into a hole. He has a selection to choose from, but he often finally uses a favourite few. The same is true of block cutting: as you work, you find, or perhaps better still make, the tool that helps you to express your ideas in print.

The strong vertical (wet bark) line is made with a strip of mahogany, saved from an old cupboard that was being hacked up. The surface is sandpapered, a double line is cut in and the dye is laid on evenly with a brush, care being taken to prevent it from creeping up the sides.

The yellow-brown flecks are difficult to cut from linoleum or wood. A furry felt gives too heavy a print; a sponge is unreliable and tends to smudge. But sponge leads me to loofah and I have to buy six, cutting a certain piece from each to make a good-sized block. Taking just the right amount of dye paste from the pad up to the loofah surface takes a lot of testing. It seems impossible to pick up a regular amount as I cannot see the pad surface nor feel the tiny wiry hairs approaching it. So I make a dabber of cloth with which to take up a small amount of dye from the pad and transfer it to the loofah (very difficult to get an even application but at least one can see what is happening). To make possible the two-colour yellow-green effect I make two dyes and two dabbers, and take a little of each every time. The linoleum block of approximately 110×350mm (4⅜×14in) is backed with 1in (25mm) hardwood. The mahogany block is of about

the same length. A long dye pad for the linoleum block is covered with two layers of calico which seem to give the right texture for the print. At this stage, sample prints can be taken to check up on block cutting edges, registration points, etc. The next job is to put the cloth down for printing.

Backing Sheet
Backing sheets were mentioned in Chapter 4. Always use a clean one. There are various ways of attaching them to the print table: this is mine.

I keep a jar of made-up Manutex gum in the refrigerator and use it for gumming down backing sheets. The recipe is:

2 litres (3½pt) water
100cc (3½fl oz) Calgon or other water softener
300g (10½oz) Manutex F

Pour the Manutex very slowly into the water, stirring all the time. Leave for twelve hours. Stir occasionally.

Take a few spoonfuls of gum and spread roughly over the waterproof surface of the print table, then with a fairly soft brush, spread as evenly and smoothly as possible – a soft hand sweeping brush is suitable. The gum is left until it is nearly but not quite dry and then the backing sheet is placed carefully over and ironed down. It is ironed from the centre, upwards and downwards and then gradually outwards, taking care not to iron in creases. The sheet is pulled gently from one side to the other until the whole surface is smoothly stretched and ironed down. It is then left to dry.

This sheet surface has many uses. It takes up surplus dye which may penetrate from the cloth being printed. Guiding lines and measurements can be drawn on it; cloth can be pinned down to it; and, above all, it is a pleasant surface on which to block print.

The length to be printed is already washed and ironed, and it is rolled up in newspaper. For this print, a finely woven but good firm cambric seemed best, and I gave it a dose of very pale tea-coloured Caledon dye so that it lost its stark whiteness.

On the backing sheet I rule a straight line parallel to the edge of the table, then unroll the cloth and lay it down beside this line. If you possess a long print table, then you can iron or pin down the whole length. Mine is not long enough, so I work from the roll, printing about a yard at a time rolling this piece in newspaper and continuing with the rest.

Ideally, designs should fit comfortably, and sometimes exactly, to repeat over the width of the cloth, and the block should be made accordingly. (In the early days this was always the case.) Today's cloths vary in width and some designs are suitable both for dress and furnishings, so a compromise is necessary to make the best possible arrangement for the future joining-up of the cloth from selvedge to selvedge. Having made this calculation, guiding lines are marked on the cloth to help keep the printing straight. If the cloth is not rolled up, a thin cotton thread can be attached to the backing from top to bottom and side to side, but I find this gets in the way of printing, and use instead tailor's chalk, a setsquare and metal rule, marking appropriate registration points accurately on the cloth.

One last tip before beginning to print. Blocks that have been used for some time for dyestuffs print better than a dry unused surface. Therefore, lay blocks face downwards on felt or blanket which has been wetted in hot water for half an hour or so. Dry off surplus water before taking up dye paste.

Printing

Always test the blocks until a clear even print can be printed and repeated. Spread just the right amount of dye paste onto the dye pad each time, brush it evenly over the pad, and then pick it up from the surface of the pad onto the block, as if it were from a pool of colour. If the block is pressed into the dye pad, then the dye is likely to creep up the sides of the block and make a badly blurred print. Check each time before printing and clean the edges if necessary. My loofah is much more tricky to print with, and is not

recommended as a solution to the problem of printing speckles.

I work from one end of the fabric, towards the other (rolled-up) end, which is on the far side of the table. I print about a metre, then cover this with paper, roll it up and continue. Some printers work from one selvedge to the other, some print in lines down the full length. I make the first print in the centre of the cloth's width and work out to one selvedge and then to the other – this is in order to keep straight. If you are a very right-handed person, as I am, or indeed left-handed, it is difficult not to allow the block to 'walk' a fraction if working always from the same direction. Printing from side to side alternately will balance up this tendency.

So, when you are satisfied that the blocks (and you) are printing well, continue on from the sample piece to the cloth to be printed. When finished and dry, roll the cloth up in paper and store it in a warm dry place. The airing cupboard is ideal. The Soledon

Plate 52 The hand block printer at work (*Richard Davies/Crafts Council*)

prints are affected by direct light, and must be kept covered. ICI's instructions include a recommendation to prolong the airing process in order to make sure that the dyestuff fully penetrates the cloth fibres. I have kept some for as long as six months, with a surprising result (see page 107). The blocks, if not immediately wanted, should be carefully washed and put somewhere flat in order to avoid warping whilst drying. Then it is on to the next print and set of appropriate blocks and pads.

Whilst working, you may well have thought of ideas for printing the blocks in a different way, introducing another colour, overprinting, or resisting parts of the design to be over-dyed later. Make notes, and, if there is any dye left over, use it up by trying out your ideas on the sample pieces. Ideas come from everywhere, all the time, and one has to catch them quickly.

We are wandering away from the first image of speckled reflections in a dark river onto sheer pattern-making with blocks of cut lines and textures, and the discovery that a block made for one purpose can be used to create another. Simply by changing colour, something different can be said.

As an example, when printing the parallel lines block (prior to the loofah one), I realised that it looked good on its own and might work well in grey on very white crisp lawn. So that went down in the ideas book and crisp white lawn was added to the cloth order.

On another occasion, I imagined this print associated with my 'Wells Cathedral steps' fabric — a cambric I had patterned with tucks, no colour or printing (see Plate 53). Why not run a tuck along the repeat line of the 'river' block? This was done, giving yet another variation which looks best with dark-printed lines on a coloured ground. Another idea was to wax — resist a line across the repeat join, then make a light stripe of tucking in between the block-

Plate 53 The author's *Wells Cathedral Steps*, a tucked and dyed cambric as displayed in her London exhibition 1961. The old French block in front is the *Hillis* spot, owned and often printed by Phyllis Barron (*John Donat*)

printed lines. This would be difficult to do and I haven't managed it yet. There is no end to all the possibilities; the problem is to choose the best and find time to do it.

The 'Wells Cathedral steps' design was inspired by the famous flight of steps to the cathedral's chapter house. They are a wonderful creamy grey, and worn over centuries into uneven but very beautiful undulating lines. I saw them as fairly closely sewn tucks on soft cambric, dyed to that pale clear grey, and I went home quickly and did it (see Plate 53). This looks very good in indigo, and I have made several lengths of

the 'steps' in indigo-dyed silk.

There is a story also behind the green/black print shown in Colour Plate 15. This is a two-block print in grassy green and brownish black on cream-coloured Irish linen. I was asked to design curtains for Leonard Elmhirst's study at Dartington Hall. The lovely room, with stone-mullioned windows, looks out onto a fourteenth-century tiltyard which the Elmhirsts restored. The steep sides, banks and jousting area are of mown grass and, on the far side half-way up the bank, are a few ancient Monterey pines. The design on the curtains reflects the shafts of sunlight through the pine needles onto the grass, and, when the curtains are drawn in the evening, they suggest the vista outside. I printed twelve floor-to-ceiling lengths on wide, furnishing width and weight, Irish linen – and wore out my arms.

7 · DYESTUFFS FOR PRINTING: RECIPES AND METHODS

The dyeing and printing of fast colours on textile fibres is a highly skilled and technical chemical business. Formerly, cloths passed through separate specialist departments, and the printing department's colours were mixed by the dye technicians in another department. One needs to know a certain amount of chemistry in order to learn how to do this oneself, and I cannot presume in a book of this size to give precise instructions. All that is possible is to indicate the method and recipe and encourage students to read and learn from the books supplied by the dyestuffs' manufacturers. It is in this spirit that the following recipes are given. One often hears, 'It won't work!' from someone trying to prepare a colour. What this really means is, 'I don't understand enough about what I am trying to do to *make* this work.' The risk of publishing recipes is that they may be taken as gospel, whereas they cannot cover all eventualities. One needs to learn the principles involved.

General Warning

Acids, alkalis, and a variety of chemicals needed for dyeing and printing are potentially *dangerous*. Do not open them until you are sure you know what to do. Read the instructions and all of the small print. If you are subject to breathing difficulties, hay fever, allergies or skin troubles, take precautions; wear a mask, rubber gloves and protective garments. Be careful, and above all learn to understand what you want to do.

Thickeners and Fixation

There are several ways in which printing colours differ from dyeing colours, and especially relevant here are thickeners and fixation treatments.

Printing with real dyestuffs may be considered as localised dyeing: in order to keep the dye colour in position, thickeners are added to the dye powder to make it into a paste. As a paste, the colour remains in position, before and during fixation. The choice of a thickening agent depends on the chemical composition of the dyestuff and type of cloth. It is important to use the recommended type or, if this is unobtainable, to get advice from the suppliers. In order to understand the intricacies of the use of thickeners, read Knecht and Fothergill on the subject, as there is too much to relate here. The recommended thickener for Soledon dyes is gum tragacanth – an excellent, smooth, easily worked thickener.

Gum tragacanth comes from the *astragalus tragacantha*, a gum tree which grows in Crete and the surrounding islands. It is supplied in the form of dry, horny scales which need to be soaked for up to three days (about 7 parts gum to 100 parts cold water), then gently boiled (preferably in a double saucepan) until a fairly thick, smooth solution is obtained. We use an Aga stove, and, if I mix the gum in the morning, by evening it can be placed in an earthenware jar in the bottom oven and left overnight. By the following morning it is ready to stir and sieve.

The above proportions will make a fairly thick solution. The mixing of it with the dyestuff is a very sensitive operation – one needs to get exactly the right consistency to spread on the dye pad. Some blocks (and one learns this by working with them) print best with a thinnish consistency of paste, others with thicker. Trials must be made.

As a substitute for gum tragacanth, Solvitose C5 may be used. This is a brand name for one of ICI's recommended thickeners for vat dyestuffs and Soledons. See *The*

Printing of Textile Fabrics by Block and Screen prepared by the ICI Dyestuffs Division, for use in colleges and schools of art.

Fixation treatments also vary according to the chemical nature of the dyestuff. Some dyes require immersion in an acid or alkaline bath, others need heat treatment from hot dry steam, which enables the print-paste mixture to combine its dyeing qualities with the cloth. It follows that, after the fixing treatment, the print-paste and any surplus dye should be washed away.

Soledon Dyestuffs

Soledon dyestuffs are stable, water-soluble leucoesters of the Durindone and Caledon vat dyestuffs. They are printed by a variety of methods and subsequently converted to the parent vat dyestuffs by oxidation in the presence of acids. (From *The Printing of Textile Fabrics by Block and Screen*, ICI).

They are light-sensitive and should therefore be protected from direct light. If the print table is close by a window, then the window should be shaded or white-washed. After printing, cloth should be placed in a warm dry area until quite dry, and left there until a fixing session is possible – the airing cupboard is ideal.

The dyestuff is usually packed in tightly lidded tins and is of a very fine powdery consistency. Take care to keep the powder dry and always to replace the lid. Urea and sodium nitrite are hydroscopic (they attract moisture), so they must be stored in airtight containers, in a dry place.

Recipe for Soledon print-paste
A recommended recipe is described in the ICI booklet (see above). After working with this for some time, I now make it in the following way.

50g (1¾oz) Soledon dyestuff
30-50cc (1-2fl oz) water at 80°C (175°F)
50g (1¾oz) urea (in the form of white crystals)
1 litre (1000cc or 35oz) prepared gum
    tragacanth
30g (1oz) sodium nitrite (half this quantity for
    Blue 2RCS)

Weigh out the required amount of dyestuff on a piece of paper on good balance scales.

Pour this into a ceramic bowl and place it in a saucepan of hot water over heat (as if you are making an egg custard). Add hot water very gradually stirring all the time. (I use a 1-1½in brush for 'stirring', as it gently 'rakes' through the powder and helps to smoothen it into a creamy paste.)

When the required amount of water has been added, heat the mixture to about 80°C (175°F), stirring (with brush) all the time. Add the urea a little at a time, then the gum tragacanth solution and finally the sodium nitrite. Stir well.

The colour of this mixture is not the final dyed colour but the intermediate 'vatting' colour (like the yellowy-green of the indigo vat), which changes in the sulphuric acid fixing bath (see opposite).

As urea is mildly hygroscopic, it helps to keep the undeveloped dyes in a suitably stable condition before fixation. It is therefore particularly useful when making strong solutions of colour, ie, when the proportion of dyestuff to liquid is high.

As a rough guide, a recipe using 30g (1oz) of dyestuff powder will print approximately 4½m (5yd) of medium-weight cotton. One learns by experience how much dye to make up for which design and type of cloth. Obviously, some patterns take up more dye than others; a small diaper or spotty pattern takes very little.

Colour mixes can be made, as with some other dyestuffs, either by weighing out the required amount of each colour, or by mixing together already made-up colour pastes. I tend to use both methods and keep records of successful mixtures. Testing for the final colour, and especially for mixtures, takes time, as you must allow the same intervals for drying, storing and fixing small samples as you would for lengths. Therefore, it may take days to obtain a special colour combination. There is no point in attempting to dry and air the samples quickly, as the dye does not then develop correctly. Other jobs can be fitted in whilst sampling is going on.

You should then plan a free day or two for the printing, since once the printing has begun, the entire length should be done as evenly as possible with no long intervals. Prepare the dye pad and print table, with backing sheet and requisite markings (see page 101). Iron the fabric ready for action, and hopefully the printing session, once begun, will proceed smoothly. When the length is finished, roll it up in newspaper or newsprint and put it in a warm dry place away from direct light. I keep about six to ten lengths before planning a fixing session.

During the early years of working with Soledons (1951 onwards), I encountered some difficulties I was not able to solve. I wrote to ICI Dyestuffs Division and received extremely helpful replies, and for many years after we had a running correspondence chiefly concerned with what was happening on a very small studio scale in contrast to the industrial quantities they were accustomed to dealing with. I learnt during this correspondence that adequate drying and allowing the prints to wait for some time before acid fixation would be beneficial. On one occasion, several months after printing, I was looking for something else in the airing cupboard and found a rolled-up length I had forgotten was there. I developed it, and there appeared a wonderful rich black – a black with some life in it. I washed and rinsed it, and put it through a soapy boil, and the colour didn't move. I had accidentally learnt how to make a Soledon black, which the ICI book said didn't exist! I wrote to them and they were of course very interested, but regretted that the process was quite unsuitable to recommend to industry at large. However, I printed a set of four large curtains (2sq yd or about 2sq m each) for south facing windows and gave them the same long-term airing in the cupboard. This was in the sixties. Eighteen years later those curtains are still unfaded. The cloth is becoming tender, as cloth does after long exposure to sun and air, and they have therefore been recently moved to face east, hoping to prolong their life even further.

Fixing bath for Soledon prints
This takes the form of a bath of sulphuric acid dissolved in water. When the printed cloth is lowered into the bath, dangerous nitrous fumes are given off. It is therefore advisable, whenever possible, to make the bath outside, or in a very well ventilated area. Stand by an open window, wear rubber gloves and be extremely careful. The recipe is as follows.

20cc (¾fl oz) sulphuric acid
1 litre (1¾pt) water at 70°C (160°F)

I make about 30 litres for a fixing session. In this amount of liquid it is possible to develop up to ten lengths in a session, and normally it can be used a second time.

Measure out the water and add to the bath (I use a strong plastic bin). Wearing rubber gloves, pour the acid very gently in a thin thread into the water, standing clear, and stir for a minute or two. Enter the cloth and move it gently for up to a minute, take it out and hold it in the air for about half a minute, then plunge it into cold water. This is the basic method, but there are additional considerations.

It is important to clear the area around the acid bath, cover the tables with newspaper and keep the lengths wrapped up until you are ready to immerse them. It is also very important that no dampness or liquid touches any portion of the printed cloth; if this happens the dried print paste will immediately spread and there is nothing you can do to remove the blemish. I keep two pairs of rubber gloves for the operation – one dry pair which is never used near the sink or acid bath, and a wet pair to change into when actually stirring the cloth around in the bath, taking it out, and plunging it into cold water.

The whole procedure is as follows. The sulphuric bath is made, the tables are covered with paper, rolls of cloth are ready, and the sinks are full of cold water. Have a smooth-ended stirring stick ready in the bath. Put on dry rubber gloves, unroll a length, carefully hold it in folds along the selvedge and enter it slowly into the bath, using the stick to push it under the surface. Do not get the gloves wet. Change into wet gloves and very gently move the cloth around with the stick and gloved hands, so that all parts receive the acid and are developed. At this stage you can see the developed colour. Do not inhale the fumes. After a minute, when all the parts are fixed, take out the cloth, hold it in the air for about half a minute and then plunge into running cold water. I have two sinks placed close together, and use both for cleansing away the sulphuric solution rinsing in one, changing the water, and rinsing in the second, until all trace and smell of sulphuric has gone. After this, the cloth is boiled in soapy water for a further five minutes. Finally, rinse and dry. This is quite a performance and can be tiring.

Finishing for Presentation

This last process is also a first – a first in the presentation of your cloth to a customer or for an exhibition. Cloth that has been roughly ironed is not acceptable.

After the final soapy washings and rinsings, immerse it for ten minutes or so in a brown sugar or molasses solution: 1tbsp to about 1gal (4.5 litres) of water (about a washing-up bowl). Allow to dry and, just before it is bone dry, iron carefully on the *reverse* side. This is important, as ironing sometimes leaves shiny marks or picks up slight impurities and spreads them on the cloth. Take no chances. Also, ironing from the back tends to reveal the weave on the front side, giving the cloth its best appearance. The sugar bath leaves the cloth soft and slightly silky.

Iron Rust for Printing

Since the primitive discovery of the colour giving properties of iron and other mineral salts (see Chapter 1), it has been found possible to localise and control the mineral by dissolving it in an acid. We learn, again from Dr Bancroft, that vegetable acids are preferred to metallic, and for a long time the acid of vinegar (alegar) was used to make what became known as iron liquor (acetate of iron). Later, a French dye chemist, Chaptal, discovered that pyroligneous acid (distilled from wood) dissolves double the quantity of iron that can be taken into solution by the strongest vinegar. There are recipes, very difficult to make nowadays, in William Partridge's *A Practical Treatise on Dying (sic)* (see Bibliography). This iron liquor was available in Barron and Larcher's day, and they used it extensively for their soft blacks and greyish browns, as can be seen in the collection at the Crafts Study Centre, Bath (see Colour Plate 2). Later on, they made an iron acid from ferrous sulphate and lead acetate. Here is their recipe.

1lb (454g) green copperas (ferrous sulphate)
½lb (227g) acetate of lead (POISON)
1qt (approx 1 litre) hot water
gum tragacanth or solvitose made very thick

Stir together the ferrous sulphate and acetate of lead with the hot water in a glass jar. (Glass is convenient as you can see the dissolution taking place.) Leave for an hour or so to settle, when the lead will have formed a precipitate (lead sulphate) as a sediment at the bottom. Above is a clear green liquid, the dyeing substance, ferrous acetate, which has to be separated from the white lead sediment. As this sediment is still in slight suspension it should not be disturbed and allowed to mix with the green ferrous acetate. Therefore, siphon off the green liquid rather than tipping the jar to pour it off. The lead precipitate is poisonous and dangerous and unfit for the drains. Ideally, it should be buried or washed down a soakaway.[1] A crust will form on the surface of the ferrous acetate, therefore, for storage, it is better to use a corked bottle than a wide-necked jar.

For printing a medium colour, mix equal quantities of ferrous acetate and gum tragacanth. As the ferrous acetate is already liquid, the gum needs to be very thick. If a paler rust colour is required, use less of rust and more gum.

After printing and drying, the stuffs should be fixed in a bath of caustic soda (sodium hydroxide) solution, made by adding ½lb (250g) caustic soda to 4gal (20 litres) water. Remember ALWAYS ADD SODA TO WATER. Mix well, work the cloth in it for about two minutes, then hang in the air to oxidize. The intermediate 'developing' colour here is dark olive-green, which must be left to oxidize to the final rust colour before finally washing and rinsing out

1 American readers should be aware that EPA regulations apply to the disposal of lead precipitate. It should under no circumstances be buried. See US suppliers for more information.

the caustic. The mineral dyes benefit from a final rinse in a molasses or brown sugar bath to soften the cloth (see opposite). See Colour Plates 3 and 9.

Iron Black

The early discoveries of a black were briefly described in Chapter 1, ie, the chemical union of tannic acid and iron. A good and manageable source of tannin was available from imported oak galls, and this is what Barron and Larcher used. The supply is unfortunately no longer available, so instead we substitute tannic-acid powder, which gives a blue rather than a brownish black. The procedure is the same in principle as in the old Indian painted textiles.

The cloth is first impregnated with a tannic-acid solution as mordant, then it is painted or printed with a paste of iron salts (ferrous acetate). The recipe calls for prior testing of the relative amounts of tannin and the strength of the iron paste, since if the iron content is too strong, the surplus will combine with the tannic mordant and dye the background as well as the print (especially on cotton, which has a natural affinity for tannic). The absorptive qualities of cloth vary, so test first on a small sample with the following quantities.

> Tannic acid equal to 2-10% of the weight of cloth to be dyed
> Warm water equal to 20 times the weight of cloth

As work proceeds, make further tests (and take notes of) the proportions of tannin to water in the preparatory soaking to achieve paler shades.

Tannic-acid powder is very fine: it needs to be mixed to a paste with a little warm water, and stirred well to remove any lumps, before slowly adding the rest of the water, still stirring (see recipe below).

The proportions of the rust printing paste should also be adjusted (see recipe). To keep the paste to a printing consistency, mix a given quantity of it in a bottle with gum and additional water. Mark these proportions on the outside and test for colour. For cotton, a very weak solution of iron gives a pleasant grey. Less iron is needed for silk. After

printing, the cloth should be steamed. As I do not possess a steamer, I keep the iron-black prints for the recommended six months before washing.

Here is a recipe for tannic black from West Surrey College of Art and Design, where steaming is available.

Tannic-acid mordant before ferrous acetate print

Calculate amounts of tannic acid (10% weight of cloth) and water (20 × weight of cloth). Slowly paste the tannic powder with a little warm water. Add the remaining water, hot, to the paste, and immerse the cloth. Ensure the cloth is below the surface – use an empty jar as a weight if necessary. Allow the cloth to absorb the tannic overnight, or longer if possible. Hang out the cloth to dry.

Do not allow the cloth to come into contact with any iron, or it will go black. Cloth mordanted in tannic can be kept for future use if stored wrapped and dry.

Ferrous acetate print to make iron black

For silk:
1 part ferrous acetate
3 parts water
4 parts gum tragacanth or Solvitose gum
For cotton:
1 part ferrous acetate
9 parts water
10 parts gum tragacanth or Solvitose

After printing allow cloth to dry; then steam for $1/2$ hour. The background can be made more yellow or buff by passing the cloth through caustic-soda (sodium hydroxide) solution before washing off.

Wash off carefully: move cloth about in cold running water, then hot water, then cold water. Dry flat.

Manganous Chloride

As stated in Chapter 1, manganous chloride is an old mineral-salt recipe for dark rich browns, very fast to light and to washing. It is fixed in a caustic-soda bath, in a similar way to iron paste and can therefore be used in conjunction with it (see opposite). In old dye books it is sometimes referred to as manganese bronze or bistre. It is supplied in pink crystals and is very hygroscopic. There are several methods: the one I use is simple.

125g (4½oz) manganous chloride
178g (4¾fl oz) hot water
178g (4¾fl oz) gum tragacanth or Solvitose
pinch of indigo carmine

Dissolve the manganous chloride in the hot water, and then add to the gum thickening. A little indigo carmine is added as a 'sightener', ie, to colour the print-paste which is almost transparent. The indigo carmine powder is not a dye and will wash out.

After printing, allow the fabric to dry and then pass it through a caustic-soda fixing bath (see page 108). Take care to ensure that there is sufficient liquid content to allow the material to be turned about freely under the surface, otherwise 'printing back' may occur if folds of the cloth touch. Ideally, you should fix cloths in full width, in a dyeing winch. After fixing, rinse and dry as for the ferrous acetate recipe (page 109).

Permanganate of Potash
(Potassium Permanganate)

This very readily gives a cool, rich brown to cloth, wood, skin and many other substances; but the colour is not fast to light and acids (see Chapter 1) and is easily removed, ie, discharged with acids. However, it affords practice in the art of printing (direct and discharge) and dyeing.

The dyestuff is produced in the form of purple crystals which take a very long time to dissolve in water. Since it gives its colour very readily and strongly to most materials it is wise to keep its stirrers, brushes and buckets labelled and apart. It is a very strong oxidizing agent and, for this reason, can be used to discharge indigo to white without having to employ a steaming process (though the method is unorthodox and difficult). The method is, briefly, to print with permanganate on the indigo, leaving an agreeable khaki colour, and to remove this in turn by immersing the whole cloth in a solution of citric acid, which discharges the permanganate. The acid does not affect any indigo untouched by permanganate. Colour Plate 17 shows an indigo-dyed cloth with printed discharged circles in white, overprinted with manganous chloride. The recipes follow.

Discharge white on indigo

This is just possible and I have used it for 2m (2yd) lengths using a block that prints only a small amount of discharge. It would be almost impossible to keep the permanganate paste in a stable enough condition to print large areas.

1tsp potassium permanganate crystals
125g (4fl oz) hot water
180-200g (6-7fl oz) thick gum tragacanth

Dissolve (it takes a long time) the permanganate in the water, then strain through a cloth into the gum and stir well. Test and be absolutely ready to use, as the permanganate will very soon oxidize and begin to destroy the gum, turning it liquid. Print as much as you can and then re-make the mixture. This is tiresome but gives a very beautiful result and is worth the trouble.

Citric-acid discharge

The above permanganate print will have partly taken out the indigo and left a khaki colour. This can be discharged with citric acid in solution (see Colour Plate 17).

8tbsp citric-acid crystals
5 litres (1 gal) warm water

Dissolve the crystals in the water, using a container large enough to enable the cloth to be easily turned and well immersed. Keep the cloth gently moving for a few minutes. If the khaki colour does not discharge to white, remove the fabric, make a stronger citric solution and add it to the bath, stirring well; then return the cloth. Obviously, if the cloth is fairly strong and of a deep indigo it may not be possible to discharge to a white unless a very strong permanganate and citric bath are used, but if the permanganate is too strong it might destroy the cotton fibres. Be careful. The most suitable cloth would be a medium weight dyed in a mid-indigo blue.

18 (*top*) Skirt length in resist-dyed indigo, with lines of machine-sewn resist and tied circles. Courtesy of Betty Daniel. (*below*) Length of painted paste-resist dyed in Soledon and overdyed in indigo. Courtesy of West Surrey College of Art and Design (*Stephen Baker*)

The excitement and value of using this method is the experience of seeing the reaction of these two colours, and the resulting creamy-white.

Following the citric-acid bath, wash the material well in cold water and then, in order to neutralise the acid, immerse it in a mild alkaline solution of sodium carbonate (washing soda).

1tbsp sodium carbonate
5 litres (1 gal) warm water

Mix well, immerse the cloth, rinse and dry.

Citric-acid discharge print-paste
A print-paste can be mixed for use on manganous chloride dyed cloth (see following chapter) to produce a white pattern

on a brown ground. Again, the strength of the citric depends on the strength of the brown. Do not attempt to take out a really strong brown unless you are satisfied with a creamy/beige discharge. Remember that mineral dyes, if used too strongly, will eventually rot the cloth. They can be used safely for medium tones.

5-10g (¼-½oz) citric-acid crystals
100cc (approx 4fl oz) warm water
approx 100cc (3½fl oz) gum tragacanth or Solvitose

Dissolve acid crystals in warm water and add slowly to an equal part of gum tragacanth or Solvitose. Print, wash, and pass through mild alkaline solution (of sodium carbonate) as above.

19 (*top left*) Dark-brown block print *Yarner*, partly waxed and overdyed in Caledon brown. Length in pale grey-green cotton dyed in Caledon, overprinted in manganous chloride (*Author*)

20 (*below left*) Brown/blue/white skirt length in cambric. Lines of stitch resist sewn by Heather Williams, dyed in Caledon brown, then unstitched and overprinted in dark-blue Soledon by the author. (*right*) Corded cotton which has been waxed, dyed in indigo, re-waxed on the blue and overdyed in Caledon (*Stephen Baker*)

8 · RESIST DYEING TECHNIQUES AND RECIPES

Tied and Sewn Resists

The general principles of resist methods are discussed in Chapter 3. To use them, we need to consider carefully the choice of cloth, colour, pattern, method and purpose. For example, delicately textured patterns can be made by gathering up selected parts of soft muslin, cotton or silk, with a very fine needle, prior to the dyeing. The thread should of course be as thin and strong as possible as it must be pulled up tightly to prevent the dye penetrating the cloth. When dyed, dried and the stitches removed, very fine subtle patterns appear from the stitching and pulling up. The level of sewing and design skill determines the result. Likewise, cloth can be pleated and bound around, tucked and stitched, and manipulated in countless ways. There is a long tradition in Japan of resist work with indigo and a handsomely illustrated book, *Shibori, The Inventive Art of Japanese Shaped Resist Dyeing* by Wada, Rice & Barten, should be studied by those interested in this fascinating technique (see Bibliography).

It was from a study of traditional cloths that the work of my group at Dartington developed; for example, in Colour Plate 8 there is a fine example of tying-in half grains of rice, and Plates 54-7 show designs made by controlled stitch-resist patterns.

Experience teaches us the most appropriate cloth to use with which size of needle and thread. The Japanese silks were exquisitely fine and sewn with a tiny needle:

Plate 54 Pleated and stitched cambric, indigo dyed by Deryn O'Connor (*Stephen Hoare*)

Plate 55 Close-up of Plate 54, clearly showing stitch marks and excellent control of vertical indigo markings (*Stephen Hoare*)

likewise the Indian muslins and diaphanous silks, whereas the Nigerian cottons are stronger and lend themselves to bold patterning. Samples and dye tests should always be made and care must be taken to calculate whether it is possible to achieve the same result on a full length as you have made on a small sample. This is not easy: sometimes it is impossible.

Stitch and tied resists are particularly appealing when dyed in indigo, a remarkably beautiful colour in all its gradations from pale to deep dark blue. Resist styles emphasise and illuminate these variations, which occur naturally in the development of the dye.

As explained in Chapter 3, there are many recipes for indigo dyeing. Here is the one Barron taught me to use. To begin with, Barron experimented with both the zinc-lime and urine vats, but the deposits proved exceedingly difficult to clear and she ran into trouble with the drains official from the local council. The sodium hydrosulphite vat was substituted and this is the one now in general use. Sodium hydrosulphite is also known as sodium diothionite in the trade. In this and the following recipes it will be referred to as hydrosulphite only.

Barron and Larcher Indigo Vat Recipe

Equipment
   12gal dustbin (approx 50 litres)
   2-3pt (1-1½ litres) basin
   stirring sticks
   spoons
   glass jar
   sacks
   newspaper
   baths or sinks for wetting out
   measuring jug
   scissors
   weights/scales

clean hanging lines
pegs
safety pins
thermometer

In the dustbin

   10gal (45.5 litres) rain water at 16°C (60°F)
   1dsp hydrosulphite

Stock solution

   3 cups sea salt
   1 cup caustic soda (sodium hydroxide) stirred
      into 1 cup water until completely dissolved
   1½ cups hydrosulphite
   2½ cups indigo grains
   2½pt (1-1½ litres) water

Solution for wetting out fabric

   2tbsp good-quality neutral detergent, eg Teepol
   1gal (4.5 litres) warm water

Fill the dustbin to within 4in (10cm) of the rim with the rain water. Sprinkle on the 1dsp of hydrosulphite, stirring gently.

Make the stock solution in a glass, ceramic or plastic basin (not metal), adding the ingredients in the order given and stirring all the time. Leave solution to stand for 5-10 minutes, when there should be a dark-purplish scum with a clear yellow liquid below it.

Lower the basin of stock solution into the vat so that it can be poured without splashing, to avoid taking air into the vat. Stir with stick right to the bottom. Leave for ½ hour.

Dip in the glass jar to take out a small quantity, look through the glass. If the liquid is yellow without any specks of blue beneath the surface the vat is ready for use. There will be a blue scum on top.

Wet the material to be dyed in the prepared warm solution and squeeze out surplus liquid. Carefully enter the material into the vat. It should be at least 2in (5cm) below the scum, so hang it by a loop of string over a rod which lies across the top. If weighted at the other end (with a stone in a bag) it will not float. First dip for 2 to 3 minutes. It will come out yellow and gradually turn blue.

Dip again for 2-3 minutes. The airing should take place over a sink or bath, not over the vat. Disturb the vat as little as possible, and keep it covered to exclude air.

After the material is quite dry, rinse in cold water. A good deal of surplus dye will come out. Finally, finish with a soapy boil.

This recipe was given to me as the one Barron and Larcher used at Painswick in the 1930s. At that time, their heyday, they had converted the stable into a printing and dyeing workshop and built a pit vat for indigo in the floor, based on specifications provided by the textile printing and dyeing firm of Turnbull and Stockdale of Accrington. (No doubt Barron had done her homework and read Knecht and Fothergill on the hydrosulphite vat and recommended methods of dyeing in it). In their vat they were able to immerse, in open width, fairly long lengths of prepared cloth.

During the dyeing procedure one learns more readily the importance of keeping the cloth below the surface of the vat, where it absorbs the colouring matter. The moment the cloth comes out of the liquid, the oxygen in the air regenerates the indigo in the pores of the cotton and turns it blue. A magical sight.

Barron taught me to make this vat in the early sixties, in a barn with much to-ing and fro-ing to find measures, jugs, sacks and hot water. Ever since that day, there have been years of excitement, frustration and fun from sharing the experience with students and friends, and having discovered a world, a life of study and interest.

Planning an Indigo Session
The line drawing of my Sigford workshop (page 76) shows that there is not nearly enough space for all the methods I have become involved with. I really need an indigo pit vat and dye kitchen all to itself. Instead, the space has to be reorganised for indigo, so I plan good long sessions. It is not worth changing everything round and turning it all blue for just a few yards of fabric.

However, one learns to manage and, if many operations take place in the one workshop, then it must be carefully organised, kept clean and tidy. For example, before a printing session, everything must be spotlessly clean, adequate amounts of dyestuff must be mixed up, and cloth prepared.

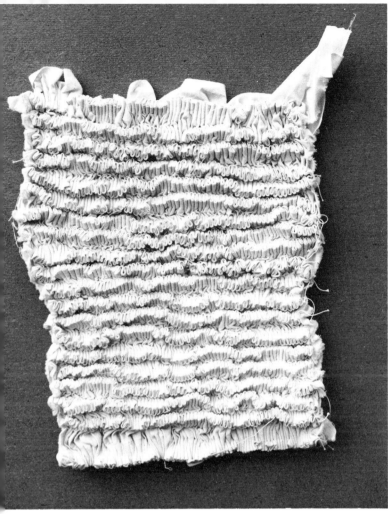

Plate 56 A 3m (3yd) length of tucked and stitched calico, prepared for dyeing in indigo by Heather Williams (*Stephen Hoare*)

Plate 57 The cloth in Plate 56 after dyeing and removal of stitches (*Stephen Hoare*)

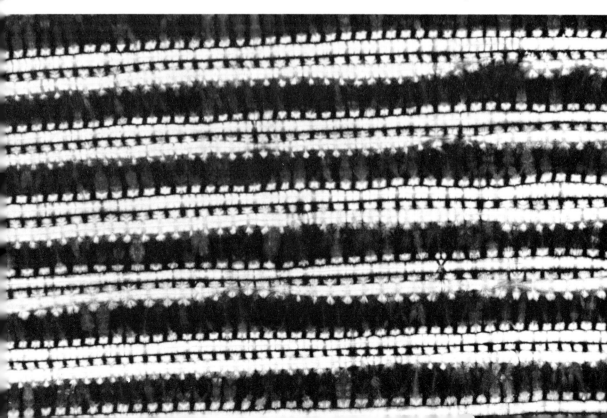

Indigo takes over everything and often fills the yard lines and shippon as well. Normally I make two or three vats in a year, and have found that the very best arrangement is to share the day with friends. In this way we all know more or less what to expect – that we shall finish up with blue faces, hands and feet, but there will be indigo cloths for all. The best time of course is a fine summer's day, bearing in mind the importance of warmth for making dyes, particularly indigo, at the right temperatures. In the past (and perhaps in a few isolated places nowadays) whole villages were given over to blue dyeing, with the family involved. In the dye factories of 100 years ago, there would have been separate workshops for plain indigo dyeing, for waxed pieces, and for special resist-printing, etc. If you decide to add indigo dyeing to other interests, then special arrangements have to be made within the one workshop.

Plan a future date and then start to estimate the number of lengths you can manage in a day. The weight and absorbency of cloth varies, eg, fine cambric takes up less dye than spongy crêpe cotton or linen. Tied and stitched pieces will take up the amount of dye able to penetrate the folds and pleats. As a guide, 15-20yd (or metres) of plain (not stitched or tied) fabric, and about the same number of stitched or tied pieces can be coped with in a day in a 10gal (45.5 litres) vat (recipe below). Normally, I would make a separate vat for waxed cloths, because, no matter how carefully the cloths are handled, little flakes of wax will float off and attach themselves to other pieces where they are not wanted, and they are very, very tiresome (sometimes impossible) to remove. As time goes on, your baskets of prepared cloths will fill up, and your friends will have prepared theirs: the day is booked.

The day before dyeing you will need to clear the workshop of printed lengths, clean cloth and all utensils and other objects that might become marked with drips of blue. Clear the floor and table tops, collect clean wooden pegs and look out the basket of plastic ones kept for indigo. Check the hanging lines and put up more if necessary. Take out long black rubber gloves for vat dyeing:

you need the industrial kind, reaching almost to the elbow, which can be obtained from builder's merchants (see Plates 5 and 46). If you have a separate wringer for blue, bring that in and take out the clean one. Sort the collection of cloths to be dyed. The plain lengths can be cut into convenient pattern pieces (if planned for garments) and the raw edges turned in and run up on the machine to prevent fraying. A tied or pleated piece might need a fishing line attached at the top edge and a stone (in a bag) attached to the bottom edge to keep it under the vat surface.

Making the Indigo Vat
Make the vat in the evening; this is how I do it now. Utensils and ingredients are as for Barron's recipe (page 115).

> 45.5 litres (10gal) water at about 25°C (80°F)
> 1kg (2lb) sea salt
> 56g (2oz) caustic soda (sodium hydroxide) flakes
> 170g (6oz) hydrosulphite
> 170-230g (6-8oz) indigo grains

Stir the sea salt gently into the water until completely dissolved. Dissolve caustic soda flakes in 2 litres (1pt) of this salted water, in a separate container. ALWAYS PUT WATER IN FIRST. NEVER POUR WATER ONTO CAUSTIC SODA. Add to vat and stir. Measure the hydrosulphite and sprinkle in slowly until dissolved. Then add the indigo grains slowly and carefully, a little at a time, stirring gently and avoiding air bubbles. (Increase the quantity of indigo to 280g (10oz) for strong blue: for medium and lighter shades, use less indigo.)

Remember that the hydrosulphite helped to take the oxygen out of the vat and, together with the caustic soda, dissolved the indigo. Do not therefore create any air bubbles, as these will weaken the colour. Stir very gently for several minutes. You will then see a brilliant-purple sheen on the surface. This is surplus indigo.

After about an hour, take a test of the colour in the clear glass jar. If it is in a good healthy state it should appear a bright greeny yellow, and a piece of paper or cloth dipped in should turn blue in a few minutes. Put the lid back on the vat and cover it up for the night. If it is winter, in an unheated workshop, then copious wrappings are necessary. Remember that indigo belongs to hot climates, that the process is one of reduction and oxidation at the right temperature. Summer is obviously the best time and one hopes to be lucky and find a good warm day for the indigo session.

In this recipe, the ingredients are added directly to the vat, whereas, in Barron's recipe, a strong stock solution is prepared first, then added slowly to the water and hydrosulphite in the vat. One advantage of Barron's method is that one can more easily ensure that all the indigo grains have thoroughly dissolved. (Note that the method of developing Caledon vat dyes, to follow, calls for this same use of a small stock solution to be prepared and gently lowered into the vat.)

Should you decide to add the ingredients straight into the dyeing vat, then be sure to stir for a very long time to make quite sure that all the indigo grains have developed before use. If they have not dissolved, dark-blue marks from the grains will inevitably appear. The same is true for mixing dye vats from powdered dyes: a long time is necessary for their complete dissolution. (I once read that commercial vats are mechanically stirred for up to fifteen minutes to dissolve powdered dyestuffs.)

Using the Indigo Vat
The morning after the vat was made, check the colour again and make final preparations. Place plastic pegs at intervals on hanging lines – this helps when hanging out dripping cloths. Cloths to be dyed should be wetted out in warm water containing a little ammonia and hydrosulphite (to accustom them to the vat liquid), and then put through the wringer.

Suppose we begin with the plain lengths. Put the long gloves on. Carefully draw the purple scum on the vat surface to one side with newspaper. Have two pairs of hands ready. Take a length, find a selvedge and, starting from one end, run your thumb and finger along it. At the same time, bunch it in the other hand, so that it is gathered into loops.

Lower the cloth carefully into the vat, avoiding bubbles, and imagine you are swimming underneath the surface, moving the cloth slowly about so that all parts of it receive an even amount of dye, without any bit surfacing to reach the air. Think of the movement of your hands, opening and gently moving the cloth in the liquid. Think all the time and the skill of doing this adroitly will be acquired. Later on you will be able to do this without thinking, and be free to talk, or think about something else.

Now, bring the cloth out of the vat, very carefully, open it and hand one end to your helper. You need to keep track of the selvedge and be quick to peg up. The air acts immediately on the cloth as it comes up and out into the air, and if there are folds these momentarily exclude the oxygen and leave pale marks. You may imagine the early dyers noticing this and puzzling out how to organise the pale and dark areas into patterns.

And so the time goes by and all the pieces have been dyed once. They will need three or four, even more, immersions, and don't forget to reverse the way you dye the plain lengths. It doesn't seem to matter quite so much for the tied-up pieces, but it is just as well to be consistent. By this time the vat, and you, will have become weary. Test the vat and, if it tends towards a bluey grey, then it is almost exhausted. It can be revived by the method below, though it may be as well to leave this for another day and finish off the dyeing session by cleaning up.

Reviving an Indigo Vat
If the vat is pale and watery, then it has gone off. Maybe all the colour has been exhausted, perhaps the proportion of caustic soda and hydrosulphite has become unbalanced and the temperature has dropped. In this case, and if another large vat is not needed for a while, then it is as well to throw the old one down the soakaway and start again. However, if there is need and the vat looks a fairly hopeful yellowy colour, then it can be revived.

The temperature should be raised to 30°C (86°F). The plastic bin cannot of course be heated on a stove, therefore the temperature will have to be raised by adding boiling water or by an immersion gadget. I have a small hand heater which I find invaluable, though I have to be careful with it (see Appendix IV for details): If the vat liquid is cloudy, add 1tbsp caustic soda, dissolved in a basin of vat liquid. If the vat liquid is on the green side, then add 1tbsp of hydrosulphite, stir very gently, leave for a while, and then test. Add a spoonful or two of indigo grains, slowly stirring continuously. Leave overnight and test the following morning. A well-made 10gal (45.5 litre) vat should last for the estimated amount of dyeing described above.

Unpicking the Ties and Washing Off

As mentioned before, colour penetration of cloth fibres (dyeing) takes a very long time to develop, so the dyed pieces are best left for as long as possible before washing off and untying. The indigo needs to oxidize completely in all parts of the fibres, and this takes longer if it is tightly woven, or folded into pleats. Leave the pieces to hang outside (or in an airy place) for at least a week – the longer the better.

There is a useful gadget, a 'Quikunpik', which is much safer than scissors for cutting tied and bound threads. Undo your sample only with this, and, if all is well, wash the full length in cold water and dry again before untying it. This is to remove surplus indigo. Finish with a very hot soapy wash, then a cold rinse followed by a weak acid bath. Rinse again and dry. For those lengths to be overdyed in a second colour, eg Caledon, wash off indigo in cold water and dry.

Tied, stitched and folding techniques for resist dyeing in indigo have been discussed and illustrated. There are other methods, eg, clamping and innumerable bindings and twistings (see Bibliography for books on *Shibori*), which await their turn for experiment. Paste as a resist for indigo is fairly difficult to manage since the ingredients and consistency have to be exactly adjusted to resist the alkaline indigo vat. My simple household flour is not suitable as the vat liquid quickly dissolves it. There are recipes in the old manuals, eg, Knecht and Fothergill, which were adapted and used by Barron and Larcher.

Caledon Dyes and Dyeing

There is a section on Caledon, Soledon and indigo vat dyestuffs towards the end of the ICI book *An Introduction to Textile Printing*, which explains very clearly their preparation and use. You will note that Caledons are very similar in some respects to indigo, eg, the dyestuff needs to be converted into a 'leuco compound', a form in which it can be dissolved to make a vatting liquid. Their solubility varies from dye to dye and for this reason you should consult the tables given in the ICI book.

The dyes are expensive and so, to begin with, I could afford only one, the Caledon Brown R (see Colour Plate 19). I already had blue in the form of the indigo vat. After working with the brown for some time it was obviously necessary to have a blue that would mix with the Caledon to cool it off and to vary the grey and buff shades. Caledon Brilliant Blue 3G powder was added and, with these, very good soft greys and light browns are possible.

Caledon Brown R

This is prepared in two parts: the dye bath, in this case a large dustbin to hold approximately 8gal (40 litres); and a smaller enamelled or stainless-steel 2pt (1 litre) saucepan in which to prepare the vatting solution. You will need a caustic-soda solution prepared by shaking 4oz (120g) caustic soda (sodium hydroxide) flakes into ¼pt (150cc) cold water until dissolved, then making up to ½pt (300cc) with more water. This is very strong and hot.

8gal (40 litres) warm water, not over 45°C (120°F)
2¾oz (80g) hydrosulphite
5½oz (150g) salt
4½fl oz (125cc) caustic-soda solution

Put water, hydrosulphite and salt into the dustbin, add the caustic-soda solution, stir gently and cover whilst preparing the vatting solution:

9fl oz (approx 200cc) hot water, at 45°C (120°F)
3½fl oz (approx 100cc) caustic-soda solution
1¾oz (50cc) hydrosulphite
3½oz (100g) Caledon dyestuff

If the dyestuff is supplied in an extremely fine powder form it is advisable to 'wet' it out first with a little methylated spirit or Turkey Red oil. Then combine the above ingredients in the basin, keeping the temperature steady. As the dyestuff dissolves, the orangey vatting colour appears. When all the ingredients are thoroughly mixed, lower the saucepan or basin into the dustbin vat and stir gently but thoroughly, and leave to settle for about an hour.

Before dyeing, wet out the cloths to assist dye penetration. Put cloths into warm water with a little mild detergent, then rinse in warm water and put through the wringer. This makes the fibres soft and more absorbent. Check the temperature of the vat and then carefully lower the pieces to be dyed, as with indigo, below the surface for 2-3 minutes. Take out and peg on the line. The air does not act on Caledons as suddenly as it does on indigo, consequently the change of colour is more gradual and even. Leave overnight, wash in warm water and finish at a soapy boil. Rinse well, dry and iron.

Mixtures of Caledon Brown and Brilliant Blue 3G give excellent shades of grey, drab, beige, dark blue, etc, particularly good over pleated and tied indigo. The sewing is left in after indigo dyeing, surplus indigo is washed off and then the piece is dyed in Caledon, which is slightly more penetrating than indigo, resulting in some of the above-mentioned colour combinations.

Other colours I have used for resist techniques include iron rust and manganous chloride.

Iron Rust Dyeing Recipe
In the old dye books this is often referred to as Iron Buff or Nankin Yellow, and there are several recipes. Here is a simple one which can be used for tied and sewn examples, but not for wax as the heat would melt it.

You will need a vitrified-enamel or stainless-steel boiling pan. An old-fashioned galvanised washing tub is possible, provided it is not chipped, as this would probably mark the cloth during the dyeing operation. All utensils for iron printing and dyeing should be kept separate as they quickly become covered with a layer of rust.

1lb (500g) ferrous sulphate crystals
1gal (4.5 litres) warm water

Add the crystals to the water and work well in until all are dissolved. Place on the heat and bring almost to boiling point. Add the wetted-out cloth and stir gently. Stir until the bath almost boils and keep stirring for 5-10 minutes. Remove and hang in the air. A greeny-gold colour appears, which gradually yellows on oxidation. When dry, pass through a caustic-soda bath, as with iron printing (see page 108). Rinse in cold water, wash in hot, then rinse in cold again, dry and iron.

The cloth is submerged in hot liquid containing a metallic dye. The heat from the stove below encourages the absorption of dye particles. It follows that, if the cloth were not stirred, that part nearest the heat would receive more dye than the other areas. Therefore, always stir gently during the absorption of the dye. In factory conditions there were rotating machines for the job. The old dye manuals recommend passing the cloth through lime water prior to the caustic-soda bath to ensure an even and softer finish.

The golden-iron colour is rich and strong. It looks particularly good with stone, wood and earthenware. A very good combination is made from a pale shade of iron dyeing, overprinted with the regular strength of iron print-paste. Manganous chloride print on pale rust is also very good. There are endless possibilities: all one needs is time. It would also be very good to have a book with all these colour samples on cloth.

Manganous Chloride Dyeing Recipe
This is again a rich colour but very difficult to dye evenly. I use it rarely as I have the Caledons, but here is a recipe.

1-3tbsp (15-50g) manganous chloride
1pt (500cc) water

Dissolve the crystals in the warm water to make up a dye bath. Immerse the cloth for about 5 minutes and hang out. When almost dry, pass through 2 per cent caustic-soda solution, rinse in cold water, wash in hot soapy water, rinse in cold and dry. Unevenness occurs in the air development, making plain dyeing difficult, but the markings are good for tie-dyeing.

The citric-acid discharge recipe (see page 110) can be used effectively on manganous-dyed cloths. Here again the permutations are innumerable. Life is not long enough.

Wax Resist

The traditional forms of wax resist techniques were discussed in Chapter 3. Similar techniques can be used with the indigo, Caledon, iron and manganous chloride dyeing described in this chapter, to make patterns of blues, greys, browns, blacks, yellows and greens in combination. Wax is a comparatively easy substance to use but needs control: there is almost nothing worse than splashes of wax passing as designs. On the other hand, intentional patterns of waxed areas or insertions of wax in block prints prior to overdyeing can produce lovely effects (see Colour Plate 20).

Wax is produced commercially in many forms, two of which are useful to us for resist dyeing, ie, paraffin wax which is hard, and beeswax which is much softer. The consistency of both can be changed with the addition of resin and oils. It really depends on what effect you are hoping to achieve. A paraffin wax will provide a 'crackled' effect as being brittle, it cracks easily when handled, allowing the dye to penetrate the fine lines. Sometimes this effect is desirable; sometimes it is not, in which case beeswax should be used as it will adhere to the cloth and bend rather than crack. Resins harden a wax mixture, and oils keep the wax fluid to assist in drawing flowing designs, and to prevent it from hardening too quickly in cold weather. Samples should be made to find the mixture most suitable for the required effect. I have a supply of partly used beeswax candles which I melt and mix with two to three parts of paraffin wax.

The heating of wax is dangerous as it will ignite of its own accord. I have a small home-made contraption for use on the Rayburn, with a fire blanket handy, but this is definitely not to be recommended. Invest in a thermostatically controlled heater which is much safer (see Appendix IV).

Depending on the type of design and cloth, a frame is very useful for stretching the cloth preparatory to waxing. It ensures that the wax settles on the cloth and not through it onto the backing material. You will need lots of newspaper and rags – always have them handy.

A *tjanting*, brush or stick can be used for applying wax. Again, tests should be made. For simple spot patterns and for filling in selected parts of a block print prior to dyeing, I use a small hogshair brush barbered to the shape I prefer.

At Alton in Hampshire, Linda Brassington runs the interesting Indigo Workshops, where metal blocks are made and printed from a heated pad of wax. Plate 58 shows a waistcoat designed, wax-resist printed and dyed in iron and indigo by Linda Brassington.

The choice of cloth depends on the final use. For scarves, ties, dress and light curtainings, poplin, cambric or calico are suitable. Wax is obviously difficult to remove from heavy cloth, or from any cloth with a pile.

Iron the cloth carefully prior to marking the design. This can be done with a soft pencil if it has been tested to wash out. Otherwise, use tailor's chalk or lines of cotton. Sit near to the heater, and learn to take up just the right amount of wax to transfer to the cloth. It should be sufficiently hot to look transparent when placed on the cloth. Work with a rag in one hand, just underneath the *tjanting* or brush to take up any spills. Cover the design with paper as you go along to avoid drips of wax. When the wax has hardened, and this does not take long, dyeing can proceed.

One cannot learn everything from a book, which can only give guidelines. It is the intimate involvement, the doing and the seeing, that counts. Look carefully and see what is happening and decide whether this or that mixture or effect is exactly what you want.

There are illustrations of the above methods. Colour Plate 20 shows how lines of wax spots have masked first the indigo dye, followed by Caledon brown, to produce white and blue spots on a brown ground. Colour Plate 19 shows the resisting of parts

of a block-printed design prior to overdyeing in brown. Colour Plate 13 shows a dark-green background with lines of wax-resisted blue circles.

Wax removal
Wax should be removed by boiling in hot water, in some cases, several times over. Never, never put hot waxy water down the sink. It will become cold, the wax will solidify and obvious troubles result. After dyeing, you can gently scrape off some wax with a spatula or back of a spoon. NEVER try to iron it out: this does not work, it just irons the wax in.

The best thing to do, and it is tiresome, is

Plate 58 Waistcoat by Linda Brassington. The collar is printed with a small metal block with wax on iron-rust-dyed calico, followed by a pale indigo dyeing to form a greenish blue. The dark areas are from iron-black dyeings on calico. The remaining creamy white areas are undyed un-bleached calico

to boil up the cloth in plenty of hot water and keep it swimming about. Do not leave it to boil – once the water is hot enough the wax melts. Take out the cloth when clear of wax, and leave the water overnight to cool off. The next morning the wax should have solidified on the surface and you can take it off, put it in newspaper which soaks up any surplus water, and save the wax for future applications. Ideally, the cloth should then be free of wax, but of course it seldom is, so the process has to be repeated. If you are lucky and have waste ground outside, dig a hole and throw the waxy water into it. Otherwise, it will have to go down the soakaway with hope that the next lot of hot water will melt any wax left in it.

As a last resort, white spirit can be used, but this again is dangerous. You could ask your local dry cleaner for help.

Waxing can give beautiful effects which cannot be achieved in any other way. It can also, unfortunately, produce hideous swirls and splodges, the fashion for which, hopefully, is passing.

Paste Resist

Having read Josef Vydra's book *L'Imprimé Indigo dans l'Art Populaire Slovaque* and seen some excellent examples of African paste-resisted indigo-dyed cloths (brought back from Abeocuta by friends), I began to try to paint lines in paste. I followed the idea, illustrated by the Nigerian ladies, who drew theirs with a small feather brush and cassava-flour paste. Being impatient, I used ordinary household flour and water mixed to a pancakey consistency and tried to draw lines on calico. The sticky paste was intractable, tiny fibres on the calico were an obstacle to painting clean lines, and I wondered whether I should have starched the cloth first. I pasted some lines but had to stop because the three children were having measles, one after another.

When finally I returned to the workshop, the calico was ruffled up and distorted, in between lines of wobbly brittle pastry. D . . . I said, and tried to pull the cloth back into shape, and in doing so I noticed tiny scissions and rippling lines in the paste. Supposing the dye could be brushed through them? Of course it could, and efforts to make a good pasting consistency of flour and to draw lines resulted in a series of linear and checked patterns, revealing the fine lacery made by pulling hardened paste.

The whole process is far too lengthy, hopelessly uneconomic but an irresistible indulgence. (It should be noted that the dye should be made up into a print-paste consistency, otherwise it would run and be impossible to control evenly.) I can see ways in which it could be developed but I must proceed with block printing and use the paste when it seems best to do so.

In the early sixties I accepted a commission from Exeter County Hall authorities to make 36yd of heavy Irish linen for curtains, patterned by stripes of brown and blue in paste resist. This had to be planned as carefully as a military exercise. The material had to be scoured, dried, ironed, cut into curtain lengths (allowances made for hems, etc), pasted and brush dyed within a given time. The dyes used were Soledons. That time had to include preparing the flour resist paste, the thickened dye, the cloth, the area to work in and a large sulphuric-acid bath, for fixing the colour. Two members of the Dartington textile group who were expert 'pasters' assisted with the lines, another helped to make up fresh paste as we used it. The cloths were resisted, dyed, dried and somehow or other, by a miracle, we managed the sulphuric-acid bath. They were then washed, rinsed, dried and ironed and sent off to be made into curtains. I don't know whether we would have welcomed a repeat order.

Removal of paste

Great care must be taken to ensure that no paste goes down the sink. Both wax and flour paste can cause considerable damage to plumbing and drainage. They should only be used in workshops where conditions allow a sensible and safe disposal. There is one safe method, and that is to judge the right time at which to scrape off the flour paste after fixing the dyestuff: with Soledons, this can be done whilst the cloth is still wet. It is difficult, but it can be scraped and brushed off by hanging the cloth on a line and working the paste downwards on to newspaper which can be burned or thrown away.

In the case of iron and manganese brush dyeing over flour paste, this can be removed after the caustic fixing bath and before the paste begins to harden. Place the cloth on newspaper and scrape the paste off, into newspaper. NEVER let the paste run down the sink.

9 · FINDING A CUSTOMER

Since the 1960s, the climate of opinion on the crafts has undoubtedly warmed, though there remain horrid cold doubts and difficulties for people wanting to set up on their own. Much can be done by studying practical guidelines and there are plenty to choose from, but their value is obviously limited and we cannot expect them to resolve the major problems since the decisions must derive from personal circumstances and philosophy – from a serious consideration of the way of life one hopes to lead. To begin with, it would seem wise to keep an open mind, as unforeseen opportunities may one day present themselves. The following remarks are intended as an indication of some of the possibilities of setting up a workshop. One cannot tell others what to do.

The decision to run a workshop includes the inevitable nightmares of selling one's work: hearts, souls and abilities are openly exposed. Who is to say one is good enough, how to find an outlet, who is going to buy, is there enough to sell, what happens if nothing sells, how to start?

Some people have worked through art colleges, others have left industry to try and go it alone, some have studied through personal experiences and research with advice from mentors. Each one of us is different, has a singular expectation of what it will mean to be self-employed, to support oneself from one's own efforts, and it is very perplexing to decide on the first moves. There are few generalisations to quantify the output of one pair of hands, since we work at different levels and tempos. The most important consideration of all is the quality of the work: if it is really good then recognition will eventually come.

Everyone's circumstances vary - one may be helped by parents or outside bodies, or not at all. One person wants to work quietly by herself, others must be in a group. One might have had the chance of studying at the RCA or other post-graduate college and have reached an eminent high standard – or not. One might have been isolated, lacking funds, stuck in a cold converted barn in far away hills making pots or tapestries of real distinction. How to reach a customer? Will anyone hear of me and buy *this*? Several years ago before the 'craft revival' the answer would have been probably not. To date the chances are legion. The puzzle is to decide the right one to aim for. If, like many, you have done well at arts and crafts at school, have worked through a foundation course and on through art college, possibly followed by post-graduate studies, it might be a wonderful idea to leave institutions behind and go off and do something you have always wanted to do but never had the time in between exams and projects and shows. Some benefit greatly from just being out in the world, doing a fairly ordinary job to keep going; and from the chance to think (away from pressures of learning), to meet different people, to travel and ponder – to put one's work into perspective.

For those whose minds are made up, there are several opportunities. Look at those in your area. If the town is preferred, the larger ones have craft galleries, centres, and people to help. There are often exhibition spaces in the library, local halls, business premises, banks, building societies, schools and colleges, and a good range of advertising possibilities. Transport and general services might be more convenient than in isolated areas, and you may prefer the bustle and activity of town life.

Some prefer a more peaceful situation and are happy to be isolated. However, one need not be seriously cut off: most counties, or

Plate 59 Fine cottons and lawns, block printed, in author's London exhibition 1961
(*John Donat*)

small area groups, have a Makers' Guild or Association. By joining you will meet others and have a chance of exhibiting regularly. There are trade fairs, craft markets and craft fairs. Go and see what they are like; who is offering what for sale, who is buying; and decide whether this is the right environment for your masterpieces. Some of the larger, well established markets and trade fairs attract buyers from far afield, from abroad, and although the pitch fee seems expensive, you have the opportunity to show to a wide variety of public and professional buyers. On a much smaller scale, and if the idea appeals, one can arrange an exhibition (perhaps with one or two other strugglers) at the local annual garden or agricultural show. It is a chance to show your work in public, to practise exhibiting, and you never know who might take notice, and buy.

You may prefer a more personal effort and organise an open day in the workshop. People are usually attracted to see inside a workshop and better still, someone at it, doing something. But this is difficult: concentration is easily lost and inspiration floats out of the window. Better not to pretend but to show to the best advantage your really good work. If these days are held regularly then there is a chance of becoming known, and of getting to know one's customers and of being recommended, through friends, to others.

Some will want to teach, to share their knowledge and expertise, others find interesting situations abroad in countries where craft skills are in need of revival and refreshment. Some are lucky, with friends who have money and prospects in large businesses and are looking for someone to provide the designs, colours and cloths they need. Another contact may put you in touch with people who look for something very different from mass-produced textiles, who want and appreciate hand printing in particular colours on special cloths. Often this can be done in discussion with the printer-dyer.

One gradually collects a range of possible designs and cloths and has to decide how much stock to keep, and what one can safely offer to do. Very often one has to face the fact that the workshop, begun in a shed or attic, just isn't large enough, isn't sufficient. One cannot make it so because there isn't any money. In the days before the Crafts Advisory Council (as it then was), we had to work on a small and hopefully steady scale, save money from here and there, accept teaching jobs and, somehow or other, manage. Today, there are possibilities for setting-up grants, and various funds for special purposes. There are many, many more openings now after training, and those whose work is of a very high standard and who want work, can find it.

A first priority, it seems to me, is to read, either by subscription or in the library, every issue of *Crafts*, the official magazine of the Crafts Council, published from 8 Waterloo Place, London, WC1. In it there are informed articles on contemporary craftspersons, details of art and craft courses, craft fairs, exhibition and selling spaces, agents, small firms, textile craft books, craft galleries, a directory of craft shops, professional advice and criticism. From the Crafts Council, there are particulars of its activities, which include grants for setting-up and special projects, bursaries and other forms of help to the needy. This will help you to understand the climate of the crafts, to read opinions. You are stimulated, infuriated, disappointed, encouraged, enlightened and fail to understand why so-and-so has shone in the limelight. If you are looking for outlets and possibilities to exhibit in a mixed or single exhibition, then there are the classified advertisements, which are always worth reading.[1]

There are of course other outlets, particularly that of design studio work and industry. I have had no personal experience but know from students and others how extremely satisfying and creative some of these jobs can be. The reverse is also true. A great deal would depend on one's individual ability to present one's work to others, to make efforts to penetrate that world, to persevere and hope that one's talents will be spotted. A sympathetic agent would obviously help to find jobs abroad and infor-

1 *Fiber Arts* and *Shuttle, Spindle and Dyepot* may serve the same purpose for American readers.

mation on international trade fairs and events. Industry *needs* highly qualified and talented young students just as badly as they need it. The difficulties in making this possible should be overcome. Public displays, representative exhibitions of students' work help to bring their potential to the notice of industrialists and design studio managers.

The Crafts Council publish authoritative booklets on many aspects of the crafts including *Setting up a Workshop* by John Crowe of the RCA. There are chapters on Finance, Points of Law, Self-Employment, Selling Work and Planning Controls. Details of this and other Crafts Council publications are in the Bibliography. The National Extension College publishes *The Small Business Kit*. CoSIRA, The Council for Small Industries in Rural Areas, is another advisory body, sponsored by the government to assist small firms in rural areas of England and Wales. It aims to help small firms to become more prosperous and so provide more employment in the countryside. CoSIRA holds evening meetings devoted to people wanting to start up. Local bank managers, businessmen and others are invited to attend. Also, CoSIRA administers loans and gives advice on constructions of small workshops.

Your local Makers' or Craft Guild will most probably arrange lectures, discussions and exhibitions which can be extremely helpful. There are a great many opportunities nowadays and organisations willing to advise on the most appropriate one for you. Good luck.

To return to the one-worker studio, there was a time in the late fifties when I felt I had sufficient work to display and was encouraged to do so. It seemed best to find a fairly large area, preferably in London, in which a personal statement and selection of work could be shown. I had not come into contact with any printers and resist-dyers, but at Dartington, where I had been teaching, the opportunity arose to work with a small, gifted group of enthusiasts. I was fortunate to have the chance of making a partnership with Annette Morel, a talented member of this group, and together we worked for

about two years on a collection to be shown in London at the Ceylon Tea Centre, Piccadilly. We approached this with trepidation on account of its size and the amount of preliminary work necessary before we could display textiles (including the installation of a false, muslin ceiling, since the existing one was vast, and too high in proportion to our needs). The exhibition included printing and resist-dyeing with paste, wax and stitching – Heather Williams being the maîtresse of the stitching.

It was all prepared in Yarner Workshop, Dartington. A model of the Tea Centre was made by Dorothy Marshall of the Royal Shakespeare Theatre who had joined us to study dyestuffs. We were able to plan exactly where each length would be hung, we inserted paper headings at the top and made hems at the bottom edge of each length, rolled it carefully in paper and packed it in its rightful position for transport. The exhibition was transported in a fleet of five Morris Travellers from Dartington to Piccadilly, to be set up over the weekend prior to 31 May 1961, for display until 10 June. We had parking spaces planned in advance, smiled at traffic wardens and managed to unpack reasonably safely. The exhibition went up as planned over the weekend and we saw one of the first performances of *West Side Story* in the evening.

We exhibited about eighty lengths and numerous made-up garments including aprons, skirts, cushions, men's ties and children's pinafores. Nearly everything was sold. Orders came from all over, from Europe, the USA, Sweden and Australia. Could we therefore contemplate the prospect of setting up a business, of taking on apprentices and/or workforce, expanding to produce hundreds of yards? No. We thought very seriously about alternatives, we took expert advice on the viable size of a small group workshop, of partnerships, profit and loss. No, we couldn't. The work had a special personal character which could not be produced en masse. If we were to take on others, however good, to do the work, it would no longer be ours, and we would be forced to change roles and become administrators. We therefore accepted as many

Plate 60 Block prints, block and wax resist, paste resist and tucked lengths in author's London exhibition, 1961 (*John Donat*)

orders as we thought we could complete and I accepted part-time teaching on specialist textile courses at Camberwell School of Art and Craft, London, at West Surrey College of Art and Design, Farnham, and Dartington College of Art.

There were, nevertheless, in a printing and dyeing workshop, jobs which could be shared by others, eg, preparatory scouring, washing and ironing of cloth, certain marking out, washings after fixation and so on. These were shared among the group and, to assist in working out costs and payments, we used a card on which each person wrote down the particular job undertaken, how long this took, and attached it to the cloth. The cloth passed through several people and, when finished, the card was passed to Annette who coped with the analysis and payment for jobs done. For the final count we added what we thought was just payment for Annette, myself and workshop overheads. Once we had decided on a charge for washing out or ironing, or whatever, we found the filling-in of cards proved an easy way of dealing with complicated job costing.

This London exhibition set a pattern for working and showing one's products which seemed more appropriate for my things than selling through shops or other marketing outlets, though they might have proved successful had we tried them. The advantages of planning one's own exhibition allow responsibility for choosing what goes in, planning the display, and the publicity. It is also a good chance to meet (and discuss the work with) visitors and clients. There are minor disadvantages mostly concerned with the time spent away from the workshop, for making agreements with the gallery management on practical matters of heating, lighting, catalogue making, printing and wardening. Some of these can be shared. I find that all this is well worth the time and trouble: one learns about exhibition designing and planning, gets a little better at it each time and has a chance to decide what line to take in the future. No one would be a block printer if she/he did not live in hope.

WORKING WITH BARRON AND LARCHER *by Enid Marx*

By 1925, at the time when I joined the Hampstead workshop of Phyllis Barron and Dorothy Larcher, their reputation was already firmly established. The work fell into a pretty regular routine, centred around the exhibitions; especially their own annual exhibition, for which new designs and special lengths were printed, and where orders were taken.

There were four of us printing in the workshop, not all at the same time as there was much else to be done: dye mixing, dyeing and all its preparations such as mordanting (and even in some instances collecting the dyestuffs, eg, walnut husks), steaming and washing. This last was an onerous job before the days of the washing machine, when everything had to be washed and rinsed a number of times by hand, much of it hosed down out of doors. Then there was ironing galore. Indeed, sometimes it seemed as if more time was taken up with the preparations than in the designing and printing. Standards were professional and comparable to those of any manufacturer, in spite of the fact that much of the equipment we used was homemade, of the 'make do and mend' variety, eg, the steamer, a converted dustbin. The blocks, too, had to be small so as to be easily handled.

In the late twenties we were experimenting with the new Chrome colours from the Swiss firm of Durand and Huguenin, whose English agents Bard and Wishart took great pains, even sending personal representatives round to give every possible help. So, for that matter, did the English firms who supplied cotton and linen, especially the three with long traditions: Warners, Morton Sundour, and Donald brothers. They were very welcoming to what they might well have spurned as amateurs or feared as rivals. On the contrary, they took the line that just because we were working on such a comparatively small scale, we were in the position to break new ground in a way that they with their factories and huge overheads could not afford to risk.

It was in the mid-twenties that Barron and Larcher were asked, through the architect Detmar Blow, to refurbish the textiles on the Duke of Westminster's yacht. So our work force was increased by two upholsterers and a needlewoman, who also made curtains and dresses for other special customers.

All this must have made a great deal of administrative work, most of which was undertaken by Barron, so ably that at the time I was unaware of just how onerous it was. Probably on account of the administrative work, much of the block cutting was done away from the workshop when we were on vacation, usually staying in Muriel Barron's cottage in France.

Looking back, I realise just how lucky we were to have been working in that halcyon period between the wars, when all the arts flowered in such profusion.

COLOUR AND THE CALICO PRINTER

In the autumn of 1982 there was an important and unique exhibition of printed and dyed textiles manufactured during 1780 to 1850, presented by the West Surrey College of Art and Design, Farnham, and later at Quarry Bank Mill, Styal, Cheshire. The aim of the exhibition was to explore and exhibit the use of dyes for printed textiles in the period up to the invention of aniline dyestuffs in 1856. This covers the period of the combination of skilful blockmaking and printing, the weaving of fine muslins, silks and velvets, and the excellence of design, culminating, with the use of the lovely madder colours, in a zenith of achievement. There were pretty day dresses, becoming skirts and jackets, delicious spotted muslins, delicate sprigged patterns, maker's design books, blocks and workshop manuals for study. An informative, illustrated catalogue written by Deryn O'Connor and Hero Granger-Taylor accompanied the exhibition and may be obtained from the West Surrey College of Art and Design, Farnham, Surrey. In it there are accurately detailed accounts of the structure of the cloths, colours and processes used; an exceptionally valuable addition to a textile library.

APPENDIX III
MUSEUMS

It is not possible to publish here a comprehensive list of contents of museums in any part of the world you might visit: much depends on what you are looking for and your own inquisitiveness. It is always worth seeking out a museum, small or large, since you never know what you may find. The following may be of help in planning your journey.

Museums and Galleries, Historic Publications, Dunstable, Bedfordshire

The Directory of Museums, Hudson and Nicholls, Macmillan

Museums Journal, 87 Charlotte Street, London, The Museums Association, 34 Bloomsbury Way, and your local reference library

Textile Museums Journal, 2320 'S' Street Northwest, Washington DC, USA

Great Britain

London The Victoria and Albert Museum, South Kensington SW7

The British Museum, Great Russell Street WC1B 3DG

The Museum of Mankind (British Museum), Burlington House W1

Bethnal Green Museum, Cambridge Heath Road E2 9PA

Geffrie Museum, Kingsland Road, London E2 8EA

Horniman Museum, London Road, Forest Hill SE23

William Morris Gallery, Lloyd Park, Walthamstow E17

Natural History and Science Museums, Exhibition Road, South Kensington SW7

Alton Jane Austen's House, Chawton, Near Alton, Hampshire

Bangor Museum of Welsh Antiquities, University College of South Wales, College Road

Bath American Museum in Britain, Claverton Manor, Claverton Down

Museum of Costume, Assembly Rooms

Crafts Study Centre Collection, Holburne of Menstrie Museum, Great Pulteney Street

Birmingham Birmingham City Museum and Art Gallery, Congreve Street

Birmingham Museum and Art Gallery, Chamberlain Square

Bristol Blaise Castle House Museum, Henbury

Bristol City Museum and Art Gallery, Queen's Road

Burnley Gawthorpe Hall, Padiham

Cambridge Fitzwilliam Museum, Trumpington Street

Dundee City Museum and Art Gallery, Albert Square

Durham Bowes Museum, Barnard Castle

Edinburgh Royal Scottish Museum, Chambers Street

Exeter Royal Albert Memorial Museum and Art Gallery, Queen Street

Glasgow Glasgow Art Gallery and Museum, Kelvingrove

Gloucester Folk Museum, Westgate Street

Guernsey Hauteville House (Victor Hugo's House), St Peter Port

Guernsey Museum and Art Gallery, Candie Gardens, St Peter Port

Halifax Bankfield Museum and Art Gallery, Akroyd Park

Hereford City Museum and Art Gallery, Broad Street

Huddersfield The Tolson Memorial Museum, Ravensknowle Park, Wakefield Rd

Ipswich Museum, High Street

Lancaster Museum, Old Town Hall, Market Square

Leeds Temple Newsome House

Lewes Anne of Cleves House, High Street, Southover

Luton Museum and Art Gallery, Wardown Park, Bedford Road
Manchester Gallery of English Costume, Platt Hall, Rusholme
Manchester Museum of Art and Crafts, The University, Oxford Road
Newcastle upon Tyne Laing Art Gallery and Museum, Higham Place
Norwich Castle Museum, Castle Meadow
Bridewell Museum of Local Industries and Rural Crafts, Bridewell Alley
Nottingham City Museum and Art Gallery, The Castle
Oxford Ashmolean Museum, Beaumont Street
Pitt Rivers Museum, South Park Road
Paisley Museum and Art Galleries, High Street
Reading Museum of English Rural Life, Whiteknights Park
St Fagan's Welsh Folk Museum, St Fagan's Castle, Cardiff
Stoke Bruerne Waterways Museum, The Canal
York York Castle Museum

Denmark
Copenhagen Museum of Industrial Art Den Permanente
National Museum of Denmark, Vestegade
Frielandsmuseek Open air Museum, Sorgenfri Station

France
Cagnes-sur-Mer Le Château, Alpes-Maritimes 06800
Paris Musée de l'Homme, Palais de Chaillot 75116
Musée des Arts Decoratifs, Pavillon de Marsan, rue du Rivoli
Louvre, rue du Rivoli
Cluny Museum, Place Painlevé, 6ème
Lyons Musée historique des Tissues, Place de la Bourse
Mulhouse Alsace Musée de l'Impression sur Étoffes, 3 rue des Bonnes Gens 68100
Nantes Musée des Arts Décoratifs, Salorges

Greece
Athens The Benaki Museum, Odos Koumbari 1, 10674

Holland
Amsterdam Rijksmuseum, Stadhouders Kade 42
Stedelyk Museum, Paulus Potterstraat 13
Tropical Museum, Linnaeusstraat 2A
Enkhuizen Zuiderzee Museum, Pepper House Headquarters
Leiden Ethnographical Museum, Steenstraat 1 2300 AE

Italy
Florence Museo Nazionale, via del Proconsolo 4, 50100 F
Rome Museo Etnografico 'Luigi Pigorini' Viale A. Lincoln, EIR 00144
Venice Correr Museum 30100

Sweden
Stockholm Statens Etnograsiska S.11527 Sto

Switzerland
Basle Museum für Völkerkunde, Augustinergasse 2, 1048
Zürich Schweizerisches Landes Museum, Museum Strasse 2, CH 8023Z

USA
New York Brooklyn Museum, Eastern Parkway New York 11238
Cooper-Hewitt Museum of Design, Smithsonian Institute, 9E 90th Street, New York City 10028
Cooper Union Museum for the Arts of Decoration, Cooper Square, New York, 10003
Metropolitan Museum of Art (and Textile Study Room), 5th Avenue and 82nd Street 10028
Museum of the American Indian, Broadway and 155 Street 10032
Museum of Contemporary Crafts, 29 West 53rd Street 10019
Museum of Primitive Art, 15 West 54th Street 10019
Boston Museum of Fine Arts, Huntingdon Avenue, Massachusetts 02115
Delaware Henry Francis du Pont Winterthur Museum, Delaware, 19735 Ohio
Los Angeles County Museum, 900 Exposition Boulevard LA 90007
San Francisco M. H. de Young Memorial

Museum, Golden Gate Park 94118 San Francisco

Shelburne Vermont Shelburne Museum

Stanford University, California The Stanford and Helen Berger Collection of William Morris textiles including the dye book from Merton Abbey works

Washington DC Smithsonian Institute, Museum of History and Technology, 20560 The Textile Museum, 2320 S Street NW 20008

Canada

Royal Ontario Museum, University of Toronto

Nova Scotia College of Art and Design 5163, Halifax B3J 3J6

India

Ahmedabad Museum of Textiles, Ahmedabad, Gujerat

New Delhi All India Handicrafts Board, Fine Arts and Crafts Society, Old Mill Road (Rafi Marg) ND 110001

Japan

Kyoto National Museum, 527 Chayamachi Higashi Yama-ku

Osaka Municipal and Fine Art Museum, Tennoji Park, Chausuyana, Tennoji-ku

Tokyo National Museum, Kokuritsu Hakubutsukan Ueno Park, Daito-ku T110

SUPPLIERS

The following list of suppliers is inevitably incomplete. Many of your queries can be solved by reading your copy of *Crafts* magazine, which contains very helpful articles, notices and classified advertisements. *Crafts* is the official magazine of the Crafts council, published from Glebe Cottage, Pear Tree Farm, Swinderby Road, North Scarle, Lincolnshire LN6 1EU. The Crafts Council is at Claremont Hall, 44a Pentonville Road, London N1 9BY.
The American Crafts Council is at 44 West 53rd St, New York 19.

Cloths
Acorn Fabrics
Union Mills, Lower Union Street
Shipton, Yorkshire

Emil Adler
23 Hillfield Court
Belsize Avenue
London W1P 7AE

Allans
56 Duke Street
London W1

Andersons
Wardley Mills, Moss Lane
Walkden
Manchester

Ascher (London) Ltd
21 Gt Castle Street
London W1

Ashton Hoare and Co
Vale Mill
Calder Vale, Garstang
Preston, Lancashire

Borovic Fabrics
16 Berwick Street
Oxford Street, London W1V 4HP

Brodie and Middleton Ltd
79 Longacre
London WC2

Garstang and Co
213 Preston New Road
Blackburn, Lancashire

Gayennes Ltd
Gayon Building, River Street
Bolton, Lancashire

Hull Traders Ltd
Pave Shed, Trawden
Colne, Lancashire BB8 8PJ

Jacer Fabrics Ltd
105 Gt Portland Street
London W1

Jones Ross and Co Ltd
18 Holly Grove
Peckham, London SE15

Livingstone Textiles Co
PO Box 5, St Michael's Lane
Bridport, Dorset BT6 3RS

McCulloch and Wallis Ltd
25-26 Dering Street, New Bond Street
London W1R 0BH

Pongee Ltd
184-186 Old Street
London EC1

Rubans de Paris Textiles
12 St Georges Street
London W1

George Weil and Sons Ltd
18 Hanson Street
London W1P 7PP

Whaley (Bradford) Ltd
Harris Court
Great Horton, Bradford
West Yorkshire BD7 4EQ

Wolfin & Son Ltd
64 Gt Titchfield Street
London W1P 7AE

Dyes and Chemicals

Boots, the chemists, may be able to help with various chemicals, mordants etc. (Chemicals can be very expensive in small quantities.)

Candlemakers Supplies
28 Blythe Road
London W14

Durham Chemicals Distributors Ltd
55–57 Glengall Road
London SE15 6NQ

Matheson Dyes and Chemicals
Marcon House, Marcon Place
London E8

The Russell Dye System
Muswell Hill Weavers
65 Rosebery Road
London N10

Townsend Chemical Works
Bramley
Leeds LS13 4ES

Yorkshire Chemicals Ltd
Kirkstall Road
Leeds LS3 1LL

Equipment

W. and T. Avery Ltd
28-30 Bernard Street
Southampton, Hampshire
Scales, weights and measures

Barlow Whitney Ltd
Process Heating Engineers
Bletchley
Milton Keynes, Buckinghamshire
Thermostatically controlled wax heaters

Bex Industrial Containers
Highams Park
London E4
High density (rigid) polythene containers suitable for chemicals and vats

Butcher's Supplies
Stokes and Dalton
Leeds 9
Heavy duty plastic containers suitable for chemicals and vats

Candlemakers Supplies
Tjantings, beeswax, paraffin wax

The Candles Shop
89 Parkway, London NW1
Beeswax and paraffin

Ganesha
6 Park Walk, Fulham Road
London, SW10
Tjantings when available

Global Village Crafts
17 St James Street
South Petherton
Somerset TA13 5BS
Tjantings when available, some plain cottons and beeswax candles

Griffin and George Ltd
Bishop Meadow Road
Loughborough
Leicestershire LE11 0RG
Immersion heaters, chemical and scientific equipment

T. N. Lawrence & Son Ltd
119 Clerkenwell Road
London EC1R 5AY
Large selection lino/wood cutting tools, hand-made paper, artists' supplies, brushes, etc

Eliza Leadbeater
Rookery Cottage, Dalefords Lane
Whitegate, Northwich
Cheshire CW8 2BN
Stainless-steel dye pots, cooking vessels and buckets

Sennelier Supplies
34 rue Lebrun 75013, Paris
Dyestuffs and dyeing containers, also small steamers for workshop use

BIBLIOGRAPHY

Adachi, Barbara *The Living Treasures of Japan* (Wildwood House, London, 1973)

Adrosko, Rita *Natural Dyes in the United States* (Smithsonian Institute Press, Washington, 1968)

Albarn, Smith, Steele & Walker *The Language of Pattern* (Thames & Hudson, 1974)

Anderson, Donald *The Art of Written Forms* (Holt, Rinehart & Winston, New York, 1968)

Anon *The Art of Dying* (sic) Trans from the German (London, 1705: subsequently republished by The Tapestry Studio, Shottery, Stratford-upon-Avon)

Baker, G. P. *Calico Painting and Printing in the East Indies in the Seventeenth and Eighteenth Centuries* (London, 1921)

Bancroft, Edward *Experimental Researches concerning the Philosophy of Permanent Colours and the best means of Producing them by Dyeing, Calico Printing etc* (Cadell & Davies, London, 1813)

Barbour, Jane & Simmonds, Doig *Adire Cloth in Nigeria* (Institute of African Studies, University of Ibadun, 1971)

Beer, Alice Baldwin *Printed Textiles in the Museum's Collection* (Cooper Union Chronicle, New York, 1963)

Bemiss, Elijah *The Dyer's Companion* (1806: republished Evert Duyckmek, New York, 1815)

Berthollet, C.L. & A.B. *Elements of the Art of Dyeing* Trans. from the French by Andrew Ure (Thomas Tegg, 1824)

Betterton, Sheila *American Textiles and Needlework* (American Museum, Bath)

Bird, F. J. *The Dyer's Handbook* (1875)

Blackshaw, H. *Dictionary of Dyeing and Textile Printing* (Newnes, 1961)

Blunt, Wilfred *The Art of Botanical Illustration* (Collins, London, 1950)

Boulger, Professor G. S. *The Uses of Plants* (1889)

Brett, Gerard *European Printed Textiles* (Victoria & Albert Museum, 1949)

Brett, K. B. 'An English Source of Indian Chintz Design' *Journal of Indian Textile History* No 1 (Ahmedabad, 1955)

Brett, K. B. 'The Flowering Tree in Indian Chintz', *Journal of Indian Textile History* No 3 (Calico Museum of Textiles, Ahmedabad, 1957)

Brett, K. B. *Bouquets in Textiles: an introduction to the textile arts* (Royal Ontario Museum, 1955)

Brett, K. B. 'The Harry Wearne Collection of Painted and Printed Textiles' *Royal Ontario Museum Bulletin* Nos 17-18 (Toronto, 1951–2)

Bridgewater, Alan & Gill *The Craft of Woodcarving* (David & Charles, Newton Abbot, 1981)

—— *Printing with Wood Blocks, Stencils and Engravings* (David & Charles, Newton Abbot, 1983 & Arco Publishing, Inc, New York)

Briggs, Asa and Shankland, Graeme (ed) *William Morris: Selected Writings and Designs* (Penguin, 1962)

Brightman, Frank & Nicholson, B. *The Oxford Book of Flowerless Plants* (OUP, 1966)

Bronson, J. & R. *The Domestic Manufacturer's Assistant and Family Directory in the Arts of Weaving and Dyeing* (Utica, 1817: reprinted Bradford & Co, 1949)

Bühler, A., Schwartz, P. R., Irwin J. *Journal of Indian Textile History* No 4 (Calico Museum of Textiles, Ahmedabad, 1959)

Bühler, Alfred *Primitive Stoffmusterungen* (Basle Museum für Völkerkunde, 1963)

—— 'Plangi-tie and dye work', *CIBA Review No 104* (June, 1954)

Calmann, Gerta *Ehret, Flower Painter Extraordinary* (Phaidon, 1977)

Camden Arts Centre *Enid Marx: A Retro-*

spective *Exhibition: Catalogue* (Camden Arts Centre, London, 1979)

Capey, Reco *The Printing of Textiles* (Chapman & Hall, 1930)

Cennini, Cennino *The Craftsman's Handbook* (Dover Publications, 1954)

Chai Fei Indigo Prints of China (Foreign Languages Press, Peking, 1956)

CIBA Reviews
'Medieval Dyeing' No 1 (1937)
'Purple' No 4 (1937)
'Scarlet' No 7 (1938)
'Cultivation of Madder' No 39 (1941)
'Madder and Turkey Red' No 39 (1941)
'Ikats' No 44 (1942)
'Plangi-tie-dye work' No 104 (1954) (Bühler)
'Indigo' No 85 (1951)
'English Chintz' No 1 (1961)
'Manchester: the Origins of Cottonopolis' No 2 (1962)

Clarke, Fiona *William Morris' Wallpapers and Chintzes* (London, 1974)

Clouzot, H & Morris, F. *Painted and Printed Fabrics, 1760–1815* (Metropolitan Museum of Art, New York, 1927)

Coates, Alice M. *The Book of Flowers – Four Centuries of Flower Illustration* (Phaidon, 1973)

Coatts, Margot *A Weaver's Life: Ethel Mairet 1872–1952* (Crafts Council with Crafts Study Centre, Bath, 1983)

Cooper, Thomas *A Practical Treatise on Dyeing and Calico Printing* (T. Dobson, 1815)

Cooper Union *Museum Chronicle* Vol 3 No 5 (1903)

Crace-Calvert, Dr F. *Dyeing and Calico Printing* (Palmer & Howe, Manchester, 1876)

Craft Study Centre *Handblock Printed Textiles, Catalogue: Phyllis Barron & Dorothy Larcher* (Holburne Museum, University of Bath, 1978)

Critchlow, Keith *Order in Space* (Thames & Hudson, 1969)

Crookes, William Sir *A Practical Handbook of Dyeing and Calico Printing* (Longmans Green, 1874)

_____ *Dyeing and Tissue Printing* (Bell & Son, London, 1882)

Crowe, John *Setting up a Workshop* (Crafts Council, London)

Damasse, J. *Sonia Delaunay – Rhythms and Colours* (Thames & Hudson, 1972)

Das, C. R. 'Tie and Dye Work', *Journal of Indian Art and Industry* (Vol 2 No 23, London, 1888)

Day, Lewis F. *Pattern and Design* (1881)

Drummond, K. *Armenian Block Printed Textiles, 14th to 19th Centuries* (1953)

Dufty, A. R. *Kelmscott; Illustrated Guide* (Society of Antiquaries, 1969)

Edelstein, Sidney *et al Dye Plants and Dyeing – A Handbook* (Brooklyn Botanic Gardens, New York, 1965)

Evans, Joan *Nature in Design: a Study in Naturalism in Decorative Art from the Bronze Age to the Renaissance* (London, 1933)

Fagg, William (ed) *The Living Arts of Nigeria* (MacMillan, New York, 1972)

Fennelly, Catherine *Textiles in New England, 1790–1840* Sturbridge Ma, 1961)

Floud, Peter 'The English Contribution to Early Textile Printing', *Journal of the Society of Dyers and Colourists* No 76 (June 1960)

_____ 'The Origins of English Calico Printing', *Journal of the Society of Dyers and Colourists* (May, 1960)

_____ 'The English Contribution to the Early History of Indigo Printing' *JSDC* (June, 1960)

_____ 'The English Contribution to the development of copper-plate printing' *JSDC* (July, 1960)

_____ *English Printed Textiles* (Victoria & Albert Museum, HMSO, 1960)

Floud, P. C. and Morris, Barbara 'English Printed Textiles' *Antiques* (March 1957 – April 1958); *The Connoisseur* (October 1957 – February 1959)

Focsa, Gheorghe *Village Arts of Romania* Exhibition catalogue (British Museum, 1971)

Forbes, R. J. *Studies in Ancient Technology, Vol 4* (London, 1956)

Gerster, Georg *Flights of Discovery* (Paddington Press, New York and London, 1978)

Grieve, M. *A Modern Herbal* 2 vols (Jonathan Cape, 1931)

Gupta, Skakti *Plant Myths and Traditions in India* (London, 1971)

Hadaway, W. S. *Cotton Painting and Printing in the Madras Presidency* (Superintendent Government Press, Madras, 1917)

Hansen, & Jones (ed) *Directory of Exhibition Spaces* (Arctic Producers Publishing, 1983)

Hargrave, Catherine *A History of Playing Cards* (Dover, New York, 1966)

Harrison, J., Irwin, J., Lowry, J., & Archer, M. *Europe and the Indies – The Era of the Companies 1600–1824* (BBC Publications, 1970)

Hatton, Richard *Handbook of Plant and Floral Ornament* (Dover, New York, 1960)

Hellot, Jean, Macquer, & LePileur d'Apligney *The Art of Dyeing Wool, Silk and Cotton* Translated from the French. (Scott Greenwood & Son, 1789)

Henderson, Philip *William Morris: His Life, Work and Friends* (Thames & Hudson, 1967)

Holstein, Jonathan *The Pieced Quilt: an American Design Tradition* (New York Graphic Society, Boston, Ma, 1973)

Holt, S. & E. *Painted & Printed Textiles from the Ninth to the Twentieth Century* (Los Angeles County Museum, 1961)

Hurry, J. B. *The Woad Plant and its Dye* (Oxford Press, 1930)

Hurst, George *Silk Dyeing, Printing and Finishing* (G. Bell & Sons, 1892)

ICI *An Introduction to Textile Printing* (Butterworths with ICI Dyestuffs Division, 1964)

_____ *Soledon Dyestuffs on Cotton* (ICI Dyestuffs Division, 1961)

Irwin, John *Art and the East India Trade* (Victoria & Albert Museum, 1970)

_____ *Batiks* (Victoria & Albert Museum, 1969)

_____ 'Indian Textiles', *The Art of India & Pakistan* (London, 1950)

Irwin, John & Brett, Katherine *Origins of Chintz, Catalogue of Indo-European Cotton Painting in the Victoria & Albert Museum & Royal Ontario Museum* (HMSO, 1970)

Irwin, John, & Hall, M. *Indian Painted and Printed Fabrics* (Ahmedabad, 1971)

Irwin, John, Pupul Jayakar *Textiles and Ornaments of India* (Museum of Modern Art, New York, 1955)

Japan Textile Color Design Centre, Tokyo *Textile Designs of Japan* 3 vols (Osaka, 1959–61)

Jayakar, Pupul *Indian Printed Textiles* (Marg Publications, Bombay)

Jones, Owen *The Grammar of Ornament* (Bernard Quaritch, 1868)

Kahlenburg, Mary H. and Berlant, Anthony *The Navajo Blanket* (Praeger Publishers with Los Angeles County Museum of Art, 1972)

Katoh, Lynn *Kimono: Artistic designs and Hand-dyeing; Significance in Colours* (Foreign Affairs of Japan, Tokyo, 1962)

Kauffman, Henry *Pennsylvania Dutch American Folk Art* (Dover, New York, 1964)

Kendrick, A. *Catalogue of Textiles from Burial Grounds in Egypt* 3 vols (HMSO for Victoria & Albert Museum 1920)

_____ 'Hand painted cottons of India' *The Connoisseur* (1926)

Knecht, Edmund, and Fothergill, James *The Principles and Practice of Textile Printing and Dyeing* (Chas Griffin & Co, London, 1912)

Knecht, Edmund, Rawson, Christopher and Lowenthal, Richard *A Manual of Dyeing* 2 vols (Chas Griffin, 1893)

Koch, Rudolph *The Book of Signs* (Dover, New York, 1930).

Kok, Annette *A Short History of the Orchil Dyes* Reprinted from *The Lichenologist* Vol 3 (1966)

Krishna, Vijay 'Flowers in Indian Textile Designs', *Journal of Indian Textile History* No 7 (Calico Museum of Textiles, Ahmedabad, 1967)

Lambert, Margaret and Marx, Enid *English Popular and Traditional Art* (Collins, 1946)

Lambert, S. *Paul Nash as Designer: Catalogue* (Victoria & Albert Museum, London, 1975)

Langewis, L. & Wagner, F. A. *Decorative Art in Indonesian Textiles* (Amsterdam, 1964)

Lawrie, L. G. *A Bibliography of Dyeing and Textile Printing* (Chapman & Hall, 1949)

Leecham, Douglas *Vegetable Dyes from North American Plants* (St Paul, USA, 1945)

Leggett, W. F. *Ancient and Medieval Dyes* (Brooklyn, New York, 1944)

Liebert, M. *Indigo MLB, Its Applications in*

Dyeing and Printing (Bradford)

Liebig, Justus von *Familiar Letters on Chemistry* (Taylor, Walton & Maberly, 1851)

McCarthy, Fiona *All Things Bright and Beautiful: Design in Britain 1830 – present day* (1972)

Mackail, J. W. *Life of William Morris* 2 vols (London, 1899)

Mailey, Jean 'Indian Textiles in the Cooper Union Museum', *Chronicle of the Museum for the Art of Decoration of the Cooper Union* Vol 2, No 5 (New York, 1953)

Mairet, Ethel *Vegetable Dyes* (Faber, 1927)

Means, P. A. *Peruvian Textiles* (Metropolitan Museum of Art, New York, 1930)

Mendes, Valerie 'Marion Dorn' *Journal of the Decorative Arts Society* (No 2, 1978)

Mitchell, Peter *European Flower Painters* (Adam & Charles Black, 1973)

Montgomery, Florence *Printed Textiles – English and American Cottons and Linens 1700–1850* (Viking Press New York, 1970: Thames & Hudson. 1970)

Mookerjee, A. *Folk Toys of India* (Calcutta, 1957)

Morris, Frances 'An Indian Hanging', *Bulletin of the Metropolitan Museum of Modern Art, New York* Vol 20 (1925)

Morris, May (ed) *The Collected Works of William Morris* 24 vols (Longmans, 1910–15)

Mortimer *Mortimer's Commercial Dictionary* Longman Howet Reese & Browne, 1819)

Morton, Alastair, & Edinburgh Weavers *Abstract Art and Textile Design* Exhibition catalogue (Scottish National Gallery of Modern Art, 1978)

Morton, James *History of the Development of Fast Dyeing and Dyes* Lecture delivered to the RSA and privately printed (1929)

Morton, Jocelyn *Three Generations in a Family Textile Firm* (Alexander Morton, 1971)

Mulhouse, Musée de l'impression sur Étoffes de Mulhouse *Raoul Dufy, Créator d'Étoffes* Catalogue (1972)

_____ *Toiles de Nantes des 18ᵉ et 19ᵉ siècles* Exhibition catalogue (1977–8)

_____ *L'Indiennage* Catalogue (1975)

Munsterberg, Hugo *Mingei: Folk Arts of Old Japan* (Asia House Gallery, 1965)

Mylius, N. *Indonesische Textilkunst: Batik Ikat und Plangi* (Museum für Völkerkunde Vienna, 1964)

Nabholz-Kartaschoff, Marie-Louise *Plangi* (Basle Museum für Völkerkunde, 1969)

_____ *Batik* (Basel Museum für Volkerkunde, 1970/71)

Napier, James *A Manual of Dyeing and Dyeing Receipts* (Charles Griffin, 1853)

Navajo Native Dyes: see Young, Stella

Nencki, Lydie *La Science des Teintures Animales et Végétales* (Dessain et Tolva, Paris, 1981)

Nigeria Magazine No 54 (Federal Government of Nigeria, 1957)

O'Connor, Deryn, & Granger-Taylor, Hero *Colour and the Calico Printer* Catalogue of an exhibition of Printed and Dyed Textiles 1750–1850 at West Surrey College of Art and Design (1982)

Oka, Hideyuki *How to wrap 5 more eggs* (Weatherhill, New York, 1975)

O'Neill, Charles *Dictionary of Calico Printing and Dyeing* (Simkin Marshall & Co, 1862)

Oprescu, George 'Peasant Art in Roumania' *The Studio* (Autumn, 1929)

Osumi, Tamezo *Printed Patterns of Asia* (Bijutsu Shuppan Sha, Tokyo; Charles E. Tuttle, Vermont, 1963)

Packer, Thomas *The Dyer's Guide* (London, 1830)

Parkes, Samuel *Chemical Essays* (London, 1815)

Partridge, William *A Practical Treatise on Dying (sic) of Woollen, Cotton & Skein silk* (H. Walker & Co, New York, 1823, Pasold Research Fund Ltd, Edington, Wilts, 1973)

Paxton, Joseph *A Pocket Botanical Dictionary* (Bradbury & Evans, London, 1849)

Pellew, Charles *Dyes and Dyeing* (Low, Marston & Co, London, 1913)

Persoz, Jean François *Traité Théorique et Pratique de l'Impression des Tissus* 2 vols (Paris, 1846)

Pettit, Florence H. *America's Indigo Blues; Resist-printed and Dyed Textiles of the Eighteenth Century* (Hastings House, New York, 1974)

Phillips, Roger *Trees in Britain, Europe & North America* (Pan Books, 1978)

Pevsner, Nicolaus *Pioneers of Modern Design from Morris to Gropius* (London, 1960)

Pliny the Elder *Historia Naturalis*, Book 35, Chapter 11 (The Bohn Classical Library, 1855)

Polunin, Oleg *Trees and Bushes of Europe* (OUP, 1976)

Potter, Edmund 'Calico Printing as an Art Manufacture' (Lecture to Society of Arts, London, 1852)

Read, Herbert *Art and Industry* (Faber, 1934)

____ *Education through Art* (Faber)

Ribeiro, A. 'A Paradise of Flowers: Flowers in English Dress in late Sixteenth and early Seventeenth Centuries' *The Connoisseur* (June, 1979)

Robinson, Stuart *A History of Printed Textiles* (Studio Vista, 1969)

____ *A History of Dyed Textiles* (Studio Vista, 1969)

Russ, Stephen *Fabric Printing by Hand* (Studio Vista, 1964)

Safford, Carleton & Bishop, Robert *America's Quilts and Coverlets* (Dutton, New York, 1972)

Sanders, T. W. *Encyclopaedia of Gardening* (W. H. & L. Collingridge, 1895 etc)

Sansone, Antonio *The Printing of Cotton Fabrics, Comprising Calico Bleaching, Printing and Dyeing* (Simpkin Marshall, 1887)

Sansone, Antonio *Dyeing and Calico Printing* 3 vols (Simkin Marshall, 1896)

Schwartz, Paul R. 'French documents on Indian cotton painting *Journal of Indian Textile History* Nos 2 & 3 (Calico Museum of Textiles, Ahmedabad, 1956 & 57)

Smith, David *The Dyer's Instructor* (London, 1850)

Storey, Joyce *Textile Printing* (Thames & Hudson, 1974)

Stutterheim, Dr W. F. *Pictorial History of Civilization in Java* (Java Institute & G. Kolf & Co, Welkevreden)

Société Industrielle de Mulhouse *Histoire documentaire de l'industrie de Mulhouse et de ses environs au XIXme siècle* (Veuve Bader et Cie, Mulhouse, 1902)

Swain, M. H. 'Turkey Red' *Scots Magazine*, Vol 82 No 6 (March, 1965)

Tanner, Heather and Robin *Wiltshire Village* (Collins, 1939)

Tanner, Robin *Woodland Plants* (R. Garton, 1982)

Thompson, Paul *The Work of William Morris* (Heinemann, 1967)

Thurston, Violetta *Ancient Decorative Textiles* (Favil Press, 1934)

____ *The Use of Vegetable Dyes for Beginners* (Dryad Press, London, 1946)

Tilke, M. *A Pictorial History of Costume* (Zwemmer, London, 1955)

Tucker, William *The Family Dyer and Scourer* (1830)

Tuer, Andrew *Japanese Stencil Designs* (Dover, New York, 1967)

Turnbull, G. *History of Calico Printing in Great Britain* (Altringham, 1951)

Ure, Dr Andrew *Dictionary of Arts Manufactures and Mines* (Appleton & Co, New York and Longmans, London, 1840)

Victoria & Albert Museum *Brief Guide to Oriental Painted, Dyed and Printed Textiles* (Victoria & Albert Museum, HMSO, 1950)

____ *From East to West* Textiles from G. P. & J. Baker. (G. P. & J. Baker, 1984)

____ *English Printed Textiles* (HMSO, 1960)

Vallance, Aymer *The Art of William Morris* (Chiswick Press, 1897)

____ *William Morris, his art, his writing and his public life* (London, 1897)

Vydra, Josef *L'Imprimé Indigo dans l'Art Populaire Slovaque* (Artia, Prague, 1954)

Wada, Rice & Barten *SHIBORI: the inventive art of Japanese shaped resist dyeing* (Kodanski International)

Ward, Mary & Neville *Home in the Twenties and Thirties* (Ian Allan, 1978)

Watkinson, Ray *William Morris as Designer* (Studio Vista, 1967)

Weir, Shelagh *Palestinian Embroidery* (British Museum, 1970)

Weyl, Hermann *Symmetry* (Princeton University, 1952)

Young, Stella *Navajo Native Dyes; their preparation and use* (US Department of the Interior; Bureau of Indian Affairs, 1940)

INDEX